Workshops for Active Learning

D1415967

John F. Parker

Vancouver Community College

For Leslie
Good Luck
John Parker
March 96

PRODUCTIONS

Delta, BC, Canada

Editor: Barbara-Anne Eddy
Typesetting and graphics: Detlef Rudolph

I wish to thank my wife, Mary, and daughter, Bobbi, for their assistance throughout the writing process; Bill Abrams, Secondary Curriculum Consultant of the Nevada School District, who continued to have faith in *Workshops for Active Learning*, and finally, my students, who have given me more workshop ideas than I've given them.

Canadian Cataloguing in Publication Data

Parker, John F. (John Frederick), 1933-
    Workshops for active learning

    ISBN 0-9694762-0-5

    1. Activity programs in education – Handbooks, manuals, etc.   I. Title.
LB1027.25.P37 1990   371.3   C90-091566-8

Other books by the author

The Writer's Workshop, second edition, 1990, Addison Wesley, Don Mills, Ontario (high school)

Writing: Process to Product, 1990, McDougal Littell, Evanston, Illinois (high school)

The Independent Writer, 1986, Harcourt Brace Jovanovich, San Diego, California and Toronto, Ontario (college)

The Process of Writing, 1983, Addison Wesley, Don Mills, Ontario (college)

The Writer's Workshop, 1982, Addison Wesley, Don Mills, Ontario (high school)

This book is dedicated to Roseanna.

Acknowledgments

"In a Station of the Metro." Ezra Pound: *Personae*. Copyright
1926 by Ezra Pound. Reprinted by permission of New Directions
Publishing Corporation. Canadian rights only.

"Spotlight on Youth – Battling a 'frightening' drop-out rate."
Andrew Hanon. Reprinted by permission of *Surrey/North Delta Now*.
June 27, 1990.

Table of Contents

PREFACE

What we're learning in our schools is not the wisdom of life. We're learning technologies, we're getting information. There's a curious reluctance on the part of faculties to indicate the life values of their subjects. (Joseph Campbell, The Power of Myth, *1988)*

In the last few years, education has often been the top news story in newspapers and magazines and on television. For instance, a 1989 episode of the CBS program *48 Hours* reported that one out of three students drops out of high school. The cameras moved into a number of classrooms to show the viewers low and high achievers. The teachers of the low achievers were able to make their courses meaningful for many of their turned-off students, persuading them to participate and take an active role in their own learning processes; the teachers of the high achievers, on the other hand, were in total control of their classes, proudly taking credit for their students' ability to parrot the facts of the course. Many of these wide-eyed, wholesome students were able to answer the questions before the teacher finished asking them.

To the viewer of this episode of *48 Hours*, it was obvious that the high achievers knew and understood all the facts of the course content after reading a textbook or listening to a well-presented lecture. The teachers of the high achievers clearly indicated that, so far as they were concerned, once their students knew the facts, they had mastered the course. But surely there is more to education than participating in drills of already known facts in a split-second question-answer quiz program. Had these high achievers been exposed to the active-learning techniques used by those teachers who were wrestling with low achievers, they would then have seen that knowing the facts means very little; it's what students do with the facts that shows their mastery of a course. If the high achievers were challenged, as the low achievers were, to analyze, apply, evaluate, and synthesize the facts, the standard of education on this continent would soar.

Barbara Walters, on another program about education, pointed out that students need to become independent thinkers instead of remaining teacher-dependent. She praised teachers who encourage high-level thinking by all students and provide opportunities for students to explore the abundance of material available for free: well-stocked libraries, newspapers, journals, members of the outside community that students can interview, and a well-organized learning community in their own classrooms.

The TV series *Learning in America* also explored education. In each program lack of money was cited as one of the many reasons for deteriorating standards. Introducing active learning into classrooms would not cost any additional money; indeed, active learning will prove cost effective. A four-color, glossy textbook or a computer for each student will not necessarily produce an independent thinker. Teachers dedicated to active learning encourage students to investigate far more sources than their textbook or a single computer program.

This text offers specific suggestions so that you can involve students in a variety of active-learning workshops. Each chapter also contains one or more blank boxes in which you can jot down your own workshop ideas that you want to apply to your specific courses.

Here are a few questions (and answers) about active learning:

What is active learning?

Based on the notion that students forget what they hear, remember a bit of what they see, but take ownership of what they do, the process of active learning encourages students to participate in a large number of different workshops on nearly a daily basis. Students, by becoming members of a learning community in their classroom, discover how to develop their high-level thinking skills.

Through active learning, poor students become competent; good students become great; and all students learn to think critically.

Why introduce active learning into classrooms?

During their first five or six years, children learn the basics of living: how to talk, eat, drink, walk, think, make choices, etc. They learn quite naturally by participating in trial-and-error activities, engaging in one-to-one discussions, imitating parents or siblings, and asking hundreds of questions. For most children, however, their learning process changes drastically when they begin their formal education and start school.

Some of the facts of our North American school and college systems deserve examination. During a typical class, a teacher speaks thirty minutes each hour; a student speaks thirty *seconds*. A student will often hear or read more than a hundred questions during one class, but seldom has the opportunity to ask a single question. To make matters worse, teachers will often answer most of their own questions within two to five seconds of asking them. Additionally, students often have to supply the answer the teacher wants, which may not necessarily be the only answer.

By contrast, in an active-learning community, once students get to know and feel comfortable with each other, those with poor study habits benefit from being with those with better habits, and those with good study habits acquire a sense of fulfilment in helping others. Within a few weeks, however, many peer groups form: the better students band together and challenge each other; the weaker ones, often helped by their peers and always helped by their teacher, improve quickly. As a result, the weaker groups begin to have a sense of worth as together they compose remarkable presentations.

How do students benefit from active learning?

Students benefit from active learning in several ways:

- In collaborating with their teacher and classmates, they discover how much they already know about a subject and what they need to know and understand.
- They find out how they must take responsibility for analyzing, applying, evaluating, and synthesizing their knowledge and understanding to make course content work for them.
- They learn how to ask as well as answer questions.

- By making connections between the course material, other subjects they are studying, and their own experiences, they make what they learn in school real and important for them.
- They become interested, independent writers, readers, speakers, and thinkers instead of being dependent on teachers.

How do teachers benefit from active learning?

The benefits for teachers are as numerous and important as those for students:

- Teachers can become partners in their students' development rather than distant, all-knowing authorities and judges.
- Because they are not presenting a lecture every period, they can devote time to individuals and small groups of students who need help or a challenge.
- With lecture time greatly reduced, or even eliminated, teachers have more time to listen to students apply independent thoughts about course material.
- As students work collaboratively, with their classmates helping to edit and evaluate their work, teachers find themselves evaluating and grading much less student work, and that work is generally of much higher quality.
- Because students are encouraged to do more thinking and take responsibility for their learning, teachers are able to complete most of their school work during school hours. Instead of taking home stacks of papers to mark and boning up on course content, teachers can begin to enjoy their new-found freedom: they can read the latest novels, take in a play or movie, go to an aerobics class, spend time with their families, devise more active-learning workshops for their students.

Research shows that teachers who mark papers in solitude and return them to the students do not significantly raise the standard of student writing. Within one-to-one tutorials, however, students are able to ask relevant questions and receive immediate answers. After such sessions, students do not repeat the same errors.

How much active learning should take place during a class period?

An active-learning devotee would say, "100%." But if you are a teacher just beginning this new approach to education, start slowly. Take from this text what you feel comfortable with. Modify it to fit your needs. Build slowly but surely. Surprisingly, some high achievers initially resist active learning, even though they probably experienced it in junior grades. In many cases, though, high achievers know how to "play the education game." They know how to become master students. They connect with the teacher, knowing how to become visible. In many cases, master students, with their teacher, engage in active-learning activities while the rest of the class sit in awe at all the erudition that goes on over their heads. As a result, the majority of students think that school means "teacher stands at the front of the room and does all the talking (or participates in discussions with a few master students), while we sit passively and listen (or daydream or do our homework or tune out)."

In a classroom that fosters active learning, there is no place for students to hide; everyone is actively involved in the learning community. For lazy or unprepared students, therefore, active learning provides more of a challenge than they are used to. If, however, teachers ease these students into the classroom learning community, they will be amazed to see turned-off students become turned on.

How does an active-learning instructor know when he or she is successful?

The successful active-learning instructor creates a learning atmosphere where the inner problems of the course content come to the surface easily and naturally for the students to solve. A body of material needs to be discovered, uncovered, liberated by everyone present. Every single student has a personal responsibility in this matter. This is an active undertaking, not a passive one. When students make discoveries themselves, those discoveries are theirs for life; this is the true measure of the success of active learning.

While writing this book, I am teaching three classes of the same English literature course. Ten years ago, in my traditional lecturer role, such an assignment would cause me no end of grief. After the third lecture on the same topic, I'd be going stir crazy. Because of active learning, however, my classes are always exciting and different – even though we are studying the same novels, films and poetry. No two classes are ever the same, even though the students participate in the same pre-viewing and post-viewing workshops on the films; the same jigsawing, highlighting, problem-solving, roleplaying workshops on the novels; the same teach-a-poem, film-a-poem activities; and the same synthesis workshops. Each class of English belongs to the students; their stamp of ownership on the course content is obvious to any observer.

Who will benefit from reading this book?

Let me qualify my answer with a large portion of humility. After teaching every grade from kindergarten to college and across the curriculum from PE to English, I still feel squeamish about suggesting to my colleagues how to teach. I think my approach may have interest because I changed from being a traditional lecturer to a dedicated active-learning instructor. I changed after a 2 1/2 year rest from near burnout, which I spent as a professional actor in London, England. Coming back into the classroom in 1980, refreshed and rejuvenated, I was determined to change my old ways and endeavor to make my students into independent rather than teacher-dependent learners. After nine years – and seven textbooks – I feel that I can offer teachers a few ideas to lessen their load, inspire their lessons, prevent future burnout, and help them to raise the level of their students' reading, writing, and thinking. So, who will benefit?

- teachers who want to try an alternative to the lecture method of teaching
- teachers who are nearing burnout
- beginning teachers
- teachers who have tried unsuccessfully to introduce active-learning workshops into their classrooms
- devotees of active learning who are always looking for an additional idea or two

At the end of one recent term, a mature student lingered behind to speak to me. When only we two were left in the room, she said, "I just wanted to let you know that I learned more in this class than all the rest of my classes put together." "Thanks," I replied. Then she added, "But you didn't teach very much, did you?" and left. I accepted her statement as a compliment.

HOW TO USE
*WORKSHOPS FOR
ACTIVE LEARNING*

I would suggest that you read through Chapter One and then dip into the other chapters as they catch your eye. Alternatively, perhaps you would like to start by reading the alphabetical list of workshops at the end of the book. If one looks interesting, turn to it.

If you are new to active learning, move slowly. Introduce only a few workshops into your lessons. Once you feel more comfortable with active learning, introduce more.

Each workshop lets you know what *Teacher Preparation* you need to do before you introduce it and the *Length of Time* it will probably take. If applicable, suggestions for *Classroom Preparation* will also appear.

DOUBLE-LINED BOXES

Chapters often contain student material within a double-lined box for you to use as you see fit. You might like to enlarge the boxed material on a photocopy machine and duplicate it for your students, or you might make a transparency of it to show on an overhead projector. If you own a copy of *Workshops for Active Learning* and use the material only in your classroom, you will not violate copyright.

The reader of all material in double-lined boxes is generally my students; therefore, you may want to adapt the material to fit your students' needs.

Finally, computer disks, compatible with WordPerfect (MS-DOS) or Microsoft Word 4 (Macintosh), of all material in double-lined boxes are available from me for $5.00 each plus 50¢ postage and handling. Having your own disk will allow you to modify and duplicate the material more easily than photocopying the text. Please refer to the last page for an order form. Remember to indicate which disk format you wish (MS-DOS or Macintosh).

SINGLE-LINED BOXES

Empty boxes appear throughout the text for you to record your own ideas for active-learning workshops. If you would care to share particularly successful ones with me, I would appreciate hearing from you. Write c/o the address at the front of the book.

Establishing a Learning Community

The ideal educational environment involves a one-on-one experience between a teacher and a student. Our most productive learning experiences probably occurred during our first five years of life with our parents. Always questioning, we learned the basics of life: eating, drinking, walking, playing, talking, sleeping, tying our shoelaces. Some of us even learned how to read, sing, memorize, play a musical instrument, solve problems, and reason.

How can we, as educators, recapture the learning environment of our first five years of life and incorporate it into our classrooms? What made learning easy and fun when we first started school? Why were we so motivated to learn?

What distinguishes us from other living creatures is our desire to learn. We must strive to establish an environment where students can question and take control of their learning processes. Motivating students within a learning community should be our goal.

Learning occurs when students are relaxed. Meeting new people, new ways, new material can easily intimidate or frighten students – no matter their age and sophistication. This section of *Workshops for Active Learning* deals with ways of helping students meet new experiences.

This section will also help you introduce students to the principles of active learning; they quickly experience the importance of belonging to a tightly knit learning community where they not only know all the others in the room but also know their strengths and weaknesses. Such a learning environment can often be as useful a resource as a roomful of books. When students hear about the interests, hobbies, and backgrounds of their fellow students, they make a mental note: "If I ever have a problem with computer science, I'll certainly ask Angie to help me," or "When I finish my term paper, I think I'll ask Richard to look it over for me." Why keep the talents of a student a secret, to be shared only with the teacher?

By the end of the first week, you might like to provide a class telephone directory. Students then realize that the support in the learning community within the classroom does not end when your class ends. Few teenage students ask their parents for advice about anything, let alone school projects, and they very often rank teachers with parents. They will, however, ask their peers to help solve highly personal problems. If students, in the classroom learning environment, have opportunities to discuss and question the value and relevancy of the learned material, they will soon discover that learning can be easy, fun, and meaningful — as it was in their first five years of life.

QUICK REFERENCE TO MOST USEFUL WORKSHOPS IN SECTION ONE

WORKSHOPS	PAGE

CHAPTER ONE

Peer Icebreakers

Imagine that you are a student about to begin a new class, eager to learn all you can about the subject. Now imagine having to walk into a classroom full of total strangers. You might feel nervous and uncomfortable, and find it difficult to think about learning.

As a teacher dedicated to active learning, what can you do to ease your students' tensions and establish a learning community in your classroom? You can begin to make learning easier and more enjoyable by involving students in some getting-to-know-you workshops.

Use your own tried and true icebreakers, or one of the workshops below. If you are fortunate enough to have a class of students who already know each other, you may choose to modify one of the workshops in order to provide a richer introduction to the course, past relationships with the subject, or some other topic you would like your students to share.

All of the workshops in this chapter encourage good listening and speaking skills. As well, you might want to try some of the workshops for icebreakers "across the curriculum" to help students synthesize their knowledge and comprehension of course material.

Continuums

Teacher Preparation: Think of appropriate topics for setting up a continuum line.

Classroom Preparation: Arrange for open space from one corner of a room to the opposite corner. (Alternatively, students can form lines around the walls.)

Length of time for one Continuum workshop: 5 minutes.

- Ask students to form a continuum line from corner to corner. You might ask them to form a continuum line according to the first letter of their first names – "A's start in this corner; Z's in that." Once they have formed the line, have everyone say his/her name in order from A to Z. Or, form a continuum using students' last or middle names. Or, use their birthdays – "January 1 in this corner; December 31 in that." For a class with many ESL students, you might use their countries of origin to form a continuum. For an adult class, use their years in the work force.

- By being involved in a different continuum line at the beginning of each class for the first several days, students get to know each other in a relaxed atmosphere.

- I often ask students to suggest additional ideas for continuum lines. They have come up with ideas like "shoe sizes," "favorite authors," "favorite sports," "where they would like to visit."

Continuums Across the Curriculum

- Instead of asking students to form personal continuums, link this workshop with course content. For example, ask students to form a line according to how interested they are in your subject – from extremely interested in one corner to completely uninterested in the other. Or form lines to answer questions such as "How good are you at spelling? reading? math? study habits? cooking? computer science? sports?"

Biog Talk

Teacher and Classroom Preparation: None needed.
Length of time: 15 to 30 minutes student preparation time; each Biog Talk takes 2 minutes.

- Ask students to find someone they do not know. Allow them time to chat. During their conversation, they should try to determine the essence of each other: what really makes the other person tick. They should not take notes while chatting; notetaking interferes with good communication. Encourage listening.
- At the end of their conversation, they should – without notes of any kind – present each other to the class in a one-minute talk. They should organize their talk around the essence of the student rather then introducing random thoughts about his or her life. They must also make sure that the rest of the class will remember the name of the student (suggest they use a mnemonic to make the student's name memorable; encourage the use of the chalkboard).
- Ask for volunteer pairs to go up to the front of the room to make their presentation. They may start by saying, "Class, I'd like to introduce you to...." When one finishes, the other begins. After each presentation, you might make a few comments – especially after the first few volunteer pairs. Compliment those who managed to bring out the essence of their subjects rather than simply providing a list of biographical facts.
- As a follow-up, you might have students compose 50-word Who's Who biographies of their subjects and post them in a conspicuous place in the classroom.

Biog Talks Across the Curriculum

- Instead of chatting to and introducing each other to the class, students should adapt personae, and interview and present characters from literature, historical personalities, scientists, artists, sports figures, etc.

A and B Visits

Teacher Preparation: You will need to prepare half as many topic questions as you have students.
Classroom Preparation: Form two circles of desks, one inside the other, with the chairs facing in opposite directions and with as much space around each pair of chairs as possible.
Length of time: Depends on your class size and whether you want everyone to get together, but give students 1 or 2 minutes for each question.

- Ask students to choose seats at random: designate students in the inner circle as **A**'s, and those in the outer circle as **B**'s.

- Pose a discussion question to the students; for example, "What are your feelings about active learning?" After each pair has discussed this question, ask all **A** students to move one desk to the right. Pose a new question; for example, "What disadvantages might occur in active learning?" Continue moving **A** students and posing new discussion questions as long as you wish. You may continue to pose questions dealing with classroom management, study habits, or personal matters.
- As a follow-up, ask the **A**'s to gather in one circle and the **B**'s in another circle. Encourage a discussion on their feelings and observations of the workshop.

A and B Visits Across the Curriculum

- Ask course content questions; for example, "Why do you think Hamlet did not kill Claudius when he had the chance?" "What is the difference between a tornado and a hurricane?" "Who had the best claim in the Pacific Northwest because of exploration by sea?" "How do you paginate a document?"

Hold a Party

Teacher Preparation: Help students plan a getting-to-know-each-other party. Have them bring food and drinks that they can enjoy throughout the party. Advise them on how to construct name tags using mnemonics to make their names memorable.

Classroom Preparation: On the day of the party, move the desks so that students can circulate freely within the room.

Length of time: 30 minutes.

- Students should circulate during most of the period, meeting all of the other students to learn their names and find out their interests, why they are taking your course, and so on. Encourage students to form pairs or trios rather than large groups. There should be lots of talk and lots of listening. If students do not voluntarily circulate, clap as a signal. Every time they hear the signal, they must circulate.
- After 15 minutes, ask the students to remove their names. Once in a while during the party, take a student aside and ask him or her to name everyone in the room. Afterwards, have the student find out any names he or she did not know.
- After 20 or so minutes, have everyone form a circle, and together name everyone in the circle. Then ask for a few volunteers who will name everyone. To their and your surprise, students will remember everyone's name.
- At the beginning of the third day of class, choose one student to name everyone. Invariably in my college English class, a few students appear on the third or fourth day of class. They are quite amazed to hear a student spouting off 30 or so names of students he or she met only the day before. The new students, of course, have to introduce themselves; they realize they've got a lot of catching up to do.

Treasure Hunting People

Teacher Preparation: Duplicate the grids below (or modify them to suit your needs).
Classroom Preparation: None needed.
Length of time: 20 minutes.

Find someone in the class who:

A. has travelled to a foreign country
B. was born in a foreign country
C. enjoys eating food from another country
D. has read at least two books by the same author
E. writes to a friend in a foreign country
F. enjoys a music group from another country
G. has worked in industry
H. has a favorite food
I. speaks a foreign language fluently
J. reads a favorite author from another country
K. is wearing something made in Japan
L. recently saw a foreign film
M. has a parent born in another country
N. is at least third generation North American

Answers

Your Name_____

Write the names & details about 14 different students; you cannot use the same classmate more than once.

A. name   country
B. name   country
C. name   food
D. name   author
E. name   address
F. name   country
G. name   job
H. name   food
I. name   language
J. name   author
K. name   article of clothing
L. name   film
M. name   country
N. name   generation

• Give each student both copies. Ask students to fill in as many blanks on the second copy as they can. If they don't finish, they can do so on their own time.

Treasure Hunting Across the Curriculum

• Students should assume personae of literary characters, historical figures, sports personalities, etc. or inanimate objects such as rocks, countries, cities, mathematical terms, etc. The object of this workshop is for students to discover as many of the personae as possible.

Who Are You?

Teacher and Classroom Preparation: None necessary.
Length of time: 5 to 10 minutes.

- Have students pair up with someone they do not know (or do not know well). Facing each other, and making eye contact, **A** asks **B**, "Who are you?" **B** responds in one or two words. After a pause, **A** repeats, "Who are you?" **B** must provide a different response. **A** pauses again, and then repeats the question for as many times as you wish. Then you should reverse the workshop so that **B** asks **A** the same question.
- Students may not find this workshop easy, but it does uncover who they really are. After the first five or six responses, students begin to search deeper and provide insightful answers to the question "Who are you?".
- As a class discussion follow-up, ask the students what they found difficult about this workshop, and why they found it difficult.
- As a writing follow-up, students might write a piece in their journals under one of these titles: "The Me Nobody Knows" or "The Me Everybody Knows."

Who Are You Across the Curriculum?
- Students should assume personæ of real or fictitious personalities or inanimate objects. **A** should ask, "Who or What are you?" until he/she is sure of the persona. **B** should dig deeper and deeper in order to provide richer responses.

YOUR OWN PEER ICEBREAKER IDEAS

Introduce Yourself

Teacher and Classroom Preparation: None needed.
Length of time: One minute per student. You can extend this workshop over two or three days, a few minutes each day.

- Ask students one at a time to introduce themselves to the rest of the class. Using no more than one minute, they should mention their name, what brought them to your class, their past experiences with your subject, their interest in the subject, their goals, other courses they are taking, and so on.
- Ask for volunteers rather than assigning a special order. Encourage students to stand at the front, sides, or back of the classroom while they introduce themselves so that everyone in the room can see them. If no one volunteers, introduce yourself. If there is a lull, introduce yourself again: "My name is...." It'll get a laugh and ease tensions. An encouraging glance from you will often inspire an unwilling or shy "volunteer."

Group Talk

Teacher Preparation: Put the following open-ended statements and questions (or adapt ones to fit your needs) on the board or a transparency.
Classroom Preparation: Students will need to get into groups of four or five in preparation for a group talk, so arrange desks or chairs in circles.
Length of Time: 10 to 15 minutes.

- Ask students to choose someone who will ensure that each person in the group gets a chance to respond to several of the statements and questions.

Group Talk on Learning

On what subject do you consider yourself an authority? (The subject may not necessarily be a school subject.)

How did you become an authority?

The best teacher I ever had was _____ because she/he...

How do you think is the best way to learn something?

How do you think is the best way to teach something?

I have/have not been involved in collaborative learning.

The benefits of collaborative learning are...

Usually I study alone/with others because...

My best school subject is _____ because...

I enjoy/don't enjoy giving an oral presentation because...

The best kind of exam is one that...

Highlights

Teacher and Classroom Preparation: None necessary.
Length of time: 15 minutes for each Highlight session.

- Depending on your needs and interest, you can present the Highlights workshop often during the term. It works well as an icebreaker, allowing students to introduce themselves to the class in a relaxed and pleasant way. It also works well for role playing, if you want students to enter the minds of literary characters, historical figures, scientific personalities, world leaders, etc.
- Although you can arrange Highlight groups any way you wish, grouping students into fours works well. Once they are in groups, they have to decide on their order of presentation: who will speak first, second, third, and fourth. During the presentation, group members should arrange themselves in a comfortable spot at the front of the room and take turns sharing their highlights.
- Vary the following specific Highlights workshops to fit your class and grade.

Personal Highlights

- This workshop works best near the beginning of the term. Students think of four different highlights in their lives that – in some way – changed their lives (for better or worse). When they have decided on the order of speakers, they should arrange themselves comfortably at the front of the room away from each other. Speaker **One** may lean against the wall, **Two** may perch on the corner of the desk, **Three** may sit on a chair, and **Four** may kneel on the floor.
- **One** begins by saying his/her name, followed by **Two**, **Three**, and **Four**. Then number **One** presents his/her first highlight. It's a good idea for the speaker to leave the comfortable spot and move freely. Each highlight should not exceed one minute and should begin by stating the year and location of the highlight. Near the end of the highlight, the student should prepare to return to the starting position. This lets **Two** know that he/she will soon be on. **Two** begins with his/her first highlight in the same manner. **Three** and **Four** follow. When **Four** finishes, number **One** presents his/her second highlight. Students may present their four highlights chronologically or climactically. The last speaker will be **Four**, presenting his/her fourth highlight. The presentation ends with **One**, **Two**, **Three**, and **Four** repeating their names.
- Depending on the tone and comfort in the room, some students will share the most fascinating, insightful, personal highlights. I've had students share details of their first love, the last time they took a drink, the last time they took drugs; one even admitted that the most significant event in her life was the day she told her mother that her uncle had been molesting her for the past fourteen years. Such sharings indicate tremendous trust in the room, bringing students closer together.
- If you feel comfortable sharing highlights in your life, feel free to take part in one or more of the groups, taking your turn in presenting four of your many highlights so that your students will get to know you better.
- In a writing class, the Personal Highlights workshop quite naturally leads to the students' writing autobiographies. In fact, presenting their highlights provides them with both content and organization.

Variations of Personal Highlights

- Instead of having students present highlights, you might suggest that they present four (or two or three) happy events, embarrassing times, angry quarrels, unhappy events, etc. Or they might select four personal goals or goals for the school term, four things they would change in the school, four things they like about school, four things they like about active learning, four ways they study, etc.
- If you sense a common problem in the room, you might like to bring it out in the open by having the class engage in one of these variations.

Highlights Across the Curriculum

- Using the same procedures as in Personal Highlights, ask students to select a literary character, an author, a historical figure, a world leader, etc. and present four highlights from that person's life.
- At times, you might like to suggest they become inanimate objects: for example, "Choose a geographical location and present four different famous attractions of that area," or "Describe a particular rock and four of its characteristics." At a recent workshop, to demonstrate how multiplication affects positive and negative numbers, four math teachers adopted the personae of the symbols **plus** and **minus**. Never comfortable with math, I finally understood how to multiply with + and –, especially after a **minus** explained how unhappy he'd be if he ever met another **minus**, because he'd lose his identity and become a **plus**. The workshop was not only a delight, but highly informative.
- In some cases, students will need more time to prepare for this workshop because they might have to do some research. Encourage students to use props or costumes if they wish; they often help both presenter and observers.
- If you wish, you might participate in the workshop as well. Choose a character that no one in a group is discussing. By participating, you can often set the tone and, in fact, offer greater details than most students are capable of. Your active participation will challenge your students to dig more deeply so that they can present a more worthwhile set of highlights of a character or author.
- Following up formal Highlights with a discussion proves invaluable. Students might also be encouraged to write their observations in their journals. Finally, students might use the results of this workshop to write a detailed character sketch.

YOUR OWN ACROSS-THE-CURRICULUM ICEBREAKER IDEAS

CHAPTER TWO

Course-Content
Icebreakers

Based on the notion that teachers should begin their classes where students *are*, not where they *think* students are or where they think students *should be*, this chapter will help you identify what your students know or don't know *before* you begin a lesson.

The following workshop will enable you to help students connect their higher-level thinking process with the course content. By providing students with the tools of higher-level thinking early in the term, you empower them to think for themselves. Workshops in Section Three deal with each aspect of the thinking process in more detail; this workshop merely introduces the taxonomy.

The sample workshop deals with a small piece of course content: a two-line poem. The content could just as easily be a math problem, a map, a painting, a complex term or anything that you want your students to know, understand, analyze, apply, evaluate, and synthesize. As you look over the workshop, modify any of the suggestions according to your needs.

Connecting the Thinking Process with Course Content

> *Teacher Preparation*: Compose open-ended statements and questions based on the course material – first, to find out how much your students already *know* about the material, and second, to enable them to apply and evaluate new material. Because these questions should lead students to the heart of the material, you need to prepare these questions and open-ended statements carefully.
>
> *Length of Time*: In order to ensure that students have a firm grasp of all the higher-level thinking skills, you might want to spend at least two hours on this workshop. Afterwards, you might repeat portions as needed.

Motivation

Length of Time: 10 to 20 minutes, depending on the sophistication of your students and the complexity of the course content material.

- On an overhead projector, project the open-ended statements and questions based on the material you want students to experience, in order to pull from them what they already know about the content.
- The following examples will prepare students not only to experience a poem, but also to identify some of the characteristics of poetry. You can either deal with these statements and questions within a full class discussion or divide the students into groups of three or four and give them a few minutes to discuss each item.

Sample questions and open-ended statements:

When I ride on a subway, I feel...
I've never been on a subway, but if I were to ride one, I would feel...
When I watch people in a packed subway, they remind me of...
When I watch a subway car speed by while I remain at the station, the people
   inside the car appear...
What would you have to do in order to focus on one person in a subway car?
If I were in a packed subway car, I would feel like a...
When a poem is said to contain "music," it...
What gives a poem rhythm?
Good poetry touches some aspect of the human condition. Which aspects of
   being human concern you most?
Can you think of a poem that has conflict? Share the poem and its conflict with
   those in your group.
Some people think that a good poem should be suspenseful. How can you create
   suspense in a poem?
A poet introduces imagery (word pictures) or figurative comparisons into a
   poem because...

- Follow up their responses with a few questions like: "Did any group not discover a response to one of the questions or open-ended statements?" If one or two groups were not able to respond, ask another group to give a response. Instead of commenting, ask the initial group if they're satisfied with the response they've just heard. If not, it's up to the answering group to provide a richer response. Of course, if no group was able to respond, everyone will be truly motivated to hear what you have to say. You will soon find out when your class is ready to proceed. (As a math student, many years ago, I never really knew what was going on in the room and, since none of my teachers discovered my difficulty, I never did catch up with the rest of the class, let alone with my math teachers.)

YOUR OWN OPEN-ENDED STATEMENTS AND QUESTIONS FOR A PIECE OF RELEVANT COURSE MATERIAL

Experience

Length of Time: 5 minutes.

- Have students form groups of three or more. If the material you want them to experience is longish, one student from the group should read it aloud while the others follow (without interrupting). If the material is extremely short, like the poem below, each member of the group should read it aloud in turn. Either on an overhead, a handout, or from a text-book, direct students to the new material. This should be the first time they experience the new material. For example:

In a Station of the Metro

by Ezra Pound

The apparition of these faces in the crowd;
Petals on a wet, black bough.

YOUR OWN MATERIAL FOR STUDENTS TO EXPERIENCE

Knowledge

Length of time: 5 to 10 minutes

- Knowing something does not necessarily mean understanding it. As children, we are able to recite nursery rhymes, the alphabet, or multiplication tables by rote, but we do not necessarily understand them. As we mature, we normally know and understand simultaneously; for many students, separating knowledge and comprehension will be difficult. But students should take the opportunity during this workshop to examine the distinct parts of their thinking process one at a time.
- You should, therefore, encourage the student groups to discuss the material until they feel that they all know it. They should then prepare a paraphrase of it (in their own words) for the rest of the class. They should not try to interpret it; only tell what is going on by stating – in their own words – what they think the text says. If no one in the group knows the meaning of a particular word, they will have to research it; for example, "apparition" in the above poem may give some students trouble.
- As a follow-up, ask someone from each group to read the collaboratively written paraphrase to the class. If you hear interpretation within a paraphrase, bring it to the class's attention.
- Ideally, each group should have come up with a paraphrase similar to "While in a station of the Metro in Paris, the faces the poet sees remind him of wet flower petals on the dark bough of a tree."
- You might wish to tell students that you give little or no credit for their knowing the material. Being able to retell the plot of a novel or identify chemical symbols isn't worth much to anyone, though it's a necessary step in the learning process; it's what they *do* with the material that determines the level of their thinking skills.
- Encourage students to use the following key words to help them know the material:

Knowledge Key Words

define
state
list
label
reproduce
paraphrase
summarize
explain in your own words
give the exact denotative meaning

Comprehension

Length of time: 10 minutes

- Students should discuss their understanding of the material, then collectively prepare a short sentence of no more than six words, stating what they think the material means. Their sentence might deal with thesis, theme, significance, or the essence of the material. They should even try to link it to some aspect of the human condition. In other words, they should show how they can read between the lines of the text. This part of the workshop encourages students to both see and understand the **subtext** of written material.

- No matter the length or complexity of the material, the sentence should never contain more than six words. Students will begin to appreciate the importance of words, especially strong verbs, in their short sentences. As each group works on its sentence, you might move from group to group to point out weak words. At this point you do not need to edit their content, merely point out weak, ineffective word choice. If groups are confused, you might steer them to discover an interpretation of the material.

- Have each group share its sentence with the rest of the class. You will soon notice that the groups will often present valid, but different, interpretations. If none come up with a valid interpretation along the lines of "Life whizzes by," you might get involved. In order for them to comprehend, you might need to lead a discussion or, with more difficult material, encourage them to do some research. At this point, you might even present a short lecture on theme, archetype, mythology, or another appropriate topic to help students read the subtext. Students should not move to the higher-level thinking skills until they fully know and comprehend the material.

- Students will be far more ready to hear and respond to your lecture if they have at least tried to understand the material on their own.

- Encourage students to use the following key words to help them understand the material:

Comprehension Key Words

separate the main point from the minor points
write a précis
summarize, explain
illustrate
interpret
read between the lines
find the main idea
write down the main claim
state the thesis of
state the theme of
give the connotative meaning of
in no more than six words, write a complete interpretation of

---

Analysis

Length of time: 20 minutes

- Once they know and comprehend the material, your students should demonstrate their ability to analyze it. By taking material apart, separating the pieces, and looking at the relationships between the pieces, they will see how the whole thing fits together: through causes and effects, effects and causes, comparisons, contrasts, chronologically, spatially, sequentially, and through other organizational methods. This analysis not only provides a general command of the material that will allow them to show their powers of higher-level thinking, but also provides – for written material – textual evidence to support their interpretation.
- When students analyze, encourage them to use the following key words to help examine the parts:

Analysis Key Words

divide, break down, dissect
identify, point out
differentiate, find the difference between
compare, contrast, compare and contrast
discover relevant information
cause, effect, cause and effect, effect and cause
classify, categorize, group, compile, arrange
outline
illustrate visually, draw
diagram

- Each person in the group should use one of the key words to make up an analysis question or discussion topic
  - that will result in an interpretation of the whole or part of the material
  - that will show how all the parts of the whole fit together
  - that will illustrate the relationship among the parts
- They should share their questions or topics with the other members of the group. Ask them to choose one, refine it, and record it on a piece of paper in order to give it to another group to answer. While they are working on this question, you might circulate from group to group to ensure that they have used at least one of the analysis key words in their question or topic. If they are analyzing literature or a passage from a textbook, they must make sure that their question or topic will lead to analysis that calls for direct reference to the text for support. NOTE: They need not know the answer themselves; in fact, it would be more helpful if they really wanted to know the answer to their question.
- If you are going to use the Ezra Pound poem, you might like to demonstrate with the following sample analysis discussion topic: "By using specific references to the text, first compare and then contrast the two lines of poetry."
- In discussion, the groups should respond to the analysis questions or topics they receive. By encouraging students to ask good questions, you empower them to analyze on their own.

- As a follow-up to the analysis of the material, have one member from each group read the analysis question or topic and their collective answer. Then, ask the group who posed the question if they are satisfied with the response. Why or why not? Be prepared for healthy discussion between the groups.
- Although important for students to master, analysis does not always allow them to get personally involved with the material. I am reminded of what the brilliant English professor, Dr. Purcell, said to one of his better students who intended to drop his course: "You mean, Mr. Callow, you want less analysis and more synthesis?" "Yes sir," was Simon Callow's reply; then, he prompt-ly left Queen's University (*Being an Actor* 24).

Application

Length of Time: 10 to 20 minutes.

- To apply, with confidence, what one already knows to new, unfamiliar material is surely a goal of any learner. Application will also help students to discover similarities and differences between previously learned material and new material.
- For example, to demonstrate their ability to apply their knowledge and understanding of the poem quoted above, I ask my students: "Imagine that you are the poet. Using your knowledge of what makes a good poem, compose a new second line for Ezra Pound's 'In a Station of the Metro.' You might, if you wish, compose a new title as well." On the overhead, I project the open-ended statements and questions from the Motivation section; while referring to statements and questions, students try to make sure their second line of poetry contains the same rhythm as the original, as well as containing music, imagery, suspense, and conflict.
- After all students have had a chance to compose their second lines of poetry, they return to their groups and choose one to share with the rest of the class. They use the established criteria contained in the Motivation statements and questions to help them choose the "best" poem.
- Here are a few examples from a recent English class; each new poem delighted the assembled audience:

> The apparition of these faces in the crowd;
> *Gems buried in the dark Earth.*

> The apparition of these faces in the crowd;
> *Colors in a rapid darkness.*

> The apparition of these faces in the crowd;
> *Blurring into shapeless speed.*

> The apparition of these faces in the crowd;
> *Flakes of snow, soon to melt.*

> The apparition of these faces in the crowd;
> *Overcooked eggs on burnt-black toast.*

- Try your own:
> The apparition of these faces in the crowd;
> ....

- For future exercises, ask each person in the group to use one of the following key words as they transfer the information contained in the material to something in their lives outside school, in another piece of material they are studying, in another course they are studying, in a future job, etc.:

Application Key Words

imagine, pretend, make believe
visualize
put yourself in the situation of
use your knowledge to
suppose
assume

- After students have completed their application questions, they should share them with their group. Then they can decide, as a group, which question to present to another group. Follow the procedure described in the Analysis section.

Evaluation

Length of time: 10 to 20 minutes.

- With the aid of your Motivation questions and statements and with their application of the material, students have probably developed a set of standards that will help them test the worth of the material. Each member of the group should use one of the following key words to evaluate both original and student-composed products:

Evaluation Key Words

rank, order, judge, grade
measure
assess, appraise
discriminate, distinguish between
select, determine, decide
support, explain
critique, criticize
recommend, suggest
convince, persuade

- You might have the whole class work together to "judge, rank, order, assess" students' application products. Or have them share individual evaluation questions (based on the original material) within their groups. They can then choose one question and pass it on to another group to answer. All groups should then share their questions and answers with the rest of the class. Discussion follows.

- If you are using the Ezra Pound poem, you might have each group determine which of the newly composed second lines meets the criteria of good poetry. Then, the "best" poet from each group might go to the front and "present" his/her poem by reading the "new" title (if one has been composed), the original line, and the new second line. The class might then rank all of the winners to determine the best poem. You might even like to compare the students' poems with the original, to see if the students think that any of their peers has the talent to be a professional poet.

Synthesis

Length of time: assign the synthesis project as homework with a 10 to 15 minute class follow-up.

- The ability to synthesize usually shows the highest level of students' thinking ability and will often produce original content. When students synthesize, they blend ideas from the material with their own thoughts and thus create or invent a new product, a new idea – which in turn others can experience, know, understand, analyze, apply, and evaluate.
- Rather than work as a group, students individually should use one of the following key words to help them create a new product:

Synthesis Key Words

combine, integrate
modify, revise
improve
rearrange, reconstruct
substitute
create, generate, devise
design, compose
plan
predict, estimate
hypothesize

- Here is a sample synthesis assignment: "Using your knowledge of what makes a good poem, create your own two-line poem on the subject of 'meeting someone fleetingly.'" Or, you might have students compose a two-line poem to synthesize their understanding of a new project the class is working on: for example, "Compose a two-line poem to demonstrate the differences between multiplication and division of fractions." or "In a two-line poem, predict the fate of life on earth if we don't stop polluting."
- Sometimes, I will ask students to display their poems around the classroom so that everyone gets a chance to read all the poems. On occasion I may have an evaluation workshop; other times, I just let the students enjoy moving from poem to poem. Many students record in their journals poems that they find effective.
- To read two-line synthesis poems on active learning, look at Couplet (Chapter 22).

Conclusion

Students emerge from these workshops with a fairly good understanding of what they need to do to think critically. They have recorded all of the key words so that they can not only distinguish an analysis question from an evaluation one, but they can also *ask* high-level thinking questions. Because the concepts in this chapter also apply to future workshops, students will quickly understand and appreciate the material in the new workshops.

Once students know how to use the key words as tools to develop their cognitive thinking skills, you will be amazed at their progress. By the way, note that nowhere in the lists of key words does the ambiguous, imprecise *discuss* occur.

YOUR OWN NOTES FOR LINKING COURSE CONTENT AND THINKING SKILLS

CHAPTER THREE

Reading Icebreakers

Many students consider their textbook a barrier rather than a help to learning. They wonder, "How can I ever get through this huge social science textbook?" or "How am I supposed to learn everything in this chemistry book?"

Probably one of the most helpful things a teacher can do is help students deal with their textbooks. Several treatments are available, but many teachers have found that the SQ3R method (described below) works well.

Look over all the workshops in this chapter to discover which you think will work best for you and your students. Because I firmly believe that I should be constantly teaching myself out of a job, I prefer the workshop, "Prereading with Open-ended Statements and Questions." Instead of working with your whole class, let them work in small groups or with partners. As a result, they will actively participate in surveying the textbook by asking each other specific questions. Modify the following suggestions to fit your textbook.

SQ3R Overview

> *Teacher Preparation*: Modify the instructions below or make up your own as a handout or overhead acetate. Ask students to form small groups to read and discuss the material.
> *Length of time*: 15 to 20 minutes.

Using SQ3R

- You read textbooks and other works (autobiographies and biographies, reference books, newspapers, magazines) mainly to discover information, either to satisfy your own curiosity or to fulfil the requirements of an assignment.

- But certainly the most important nonfiction you read as a student will be textbooks, and the more effectively and skillfully you can extract from them the information you need, the better equipped you will be for success in your studies. Here are some strategies to help you discover what textbooks can offer you:

Get the Complete Picture

- As a group, decide on a textbook that you would like to use to follow the steps outlined here. They may not all necessarily apply to your chosen textbook, but they will surely apply to other textbooks that you survey.

  Almost all textbooks have a table of contents, outlining what sort of information the text contains. The table of contents lists main chapter headings, and sometimes subheadings, to let you know what each chapter contains. The table of contents will also list other material in the book (preface, appendixes, glossary, bibliography, index).

⇨

Turn to the Table of Contents of your chosen textbook. How many chapters does it contain? How many appendixes? Is there a glossary, bibliography, or index? What sort of material do you find in the preface? the glossary? the bibliography? the index?

Zero In

• By consulting the table of contents, as well as the index and glossary (if applicable), you will discover where to seek the information you need. You should have no trouble consulting a single page to find out what you need to know, but if you need to locate and extract a lot of information, you will find a reading strategy such as SQ3R useful.

SQ3R

• You may already be familiar with the reading process called SQ3R (Survey, Question, Read, Recite, Review). It was especially developed to help students gain the greatest possible benefit from reading textbooks. Here is a brief summary of the technique. As you read it aloud within your group, ask questions of each other if you do not understand a particular point.

a) **Survey**   Read only the title and headings or subheadings of a chapter, as well as the opening and closing paragraphs. Note whether the chapter or section contains pictures, diagrams, or other illustrative material.

b) **Question**   Compose questions based on the title and main headings. For example, after reading a title, you may ask, "What does that mean?" Also, question the author's use of material: "What is he or she trying to say? How? Why? Why did the author include this picture? What has it to do with the content of this chapter?"

c) **Read**   Here you do your main reading of the chapter or section, discovering the details of its contents and what useful information it contains. Use the questions you have already composed as a starting point, reading carefully the passages that contain the answers to those questions and omitting or reading quickly those that do not. If you find some essential passages difficult to understand, reread them slowly, ask your group for help, and try to paraphrase them so that you *know* what the author is saying.

d) **Recite**   Reciting (talking or writing about what you have read) reinforces your grasp of the information you have gained and helps you remember it. During this time, you should think about the subtext to determine whether you completely understand what you have read. Writing in your journal and talking to the members of your group are invaluable aids in your reciting process in making the information you have read truly yours.

e) **Review**   You will usually review textbook material in preparation for a test; however, you should also try to review it throughout the term so that you are fully acquainted with it and do not need to "cram" the night before a test. Use the following suggestions for reviewing a textbook:
  • Quickly reread the material, along with your questions and answers and any journal entries you made.
  • Discuss it with another member of your group or a friend.
  • Write a 25-word summary of particular passages.[*]
  • Make up possible exam questions about the material (or have the members of your group do so) and answer them.[**]

---

[*] See Chapter 17 for details.
[**] See Chapter 6 for details on making up exam questions.

SQ3R Textbook

Teacher Preparation: Modify the instructions below or make up your own as a handout or overhead acetate.
Length of time: 25 to 30 minutes.

Examining Your Textbook

Within a group of three or four, answer the following questions about your chosen textbook:

- What is the significance of the cover design?
- If there is a Note to Students, what is its main message? Summarize it in exactly 25 words. If there is a Note to Instructors, should students read it? Why?
- How many sections does the textbook have? What is the main feature and purpose of each section? What are the differences between the sections?
- How many chapters are there? Are there subheadings? What does each chapter contain? Which chapter(s) do you think are most important? Why?
- If there is a glossary, how will you find it useful?
- How is the index organized? Is it cross-referenced?
- Find the acknowledgments. Why are they included in the textbook?
- Are there suggested answers anywhere in the textbook? How should you deal with them?
- If you want to consult another book for further information on a particular subject that is giving you trouble, does the textbook direct you to other books? Where?
- Does the book contain illustrations? Why?
- How many colors are used to print the book? Why were the colors chosen?
- Open the book in the middle. Look at the top of each page. Is the information on the top of the left-hand page different from that on the right? What is different? How does the information help you move around the book quickly?

Reading with a Pencil

Teacher Preparation: Prepare questions and suggestions on a handout or overhead acetate.
Length of Time: 20 minutes.

- In his essay, "Of Studies," Francis Bacon said that "some books are to be tasted, others to be swallowed, and some few to be chewed and digested." Certainly textbooks should fall into the last category. In order to "digest" textbooks, students need to interact with them, combining their own knowledge with what they discover in the books to yield a new and marvelous product: an enlightened student.
- But one obstacle prevents students from interacting with textbooks: generally the same books must be used year after year, and students who mark up their books may have to pay for replacements. Teachers must try to convince administrators that textbooks are learning tools, meant to be used in the same way as pencils, paper, and other tools. After all, we don't give students pencils and say, "Return them in perfect condition." In fact, we expect them

to use them. If marking in textbooks is strictly forbidden, you might ask students to write on Post It notes instead of in the book, sticking each note near the place on the page to which it refers.

Pencil Reading

As you read a chapter from the textbook, react in pencil in the margins:
  • ask questions of the author about material that confuses you (if you cannot find the answer in a later part of the textbook, ask your peers or me)
  • indicate if you already knew what you've just read
  • compliment the author on particular parts of the text that you like best, explaining why you like them
  • comment on the use of particular illustrations or photographs
  • cross-reference to other parts of the textbook if you see links
  • cross-reference to other courses if the material is relevant to them
  • provide further details from lectures or information you already know
  • signify that you've just learned something (say "I got it!")
  • register parts that you think will be important to remember
  • focus on parts that are confusing you so that you can go over them with a peer

---

Prereading with Open-ended Statements and Questions

Teacher and Classroom Preparation: After the first two chapters from any textbook, none required. Students will be actively involved in "teaching" the textbook.
Length of Time per workshop: 10 minutes

  • Instead of assuming that your students know nothing about a particular chapter in a textbook and assigning students to read that chapter for a future class, you might engage students in a ten-minute workshop to determine what they already know about the material in the chapter before they read it. Modify the workshop below to fit your textbook.
  • Have students get into groups of three or four. Have them appoint a leader who will be responsible for seeing that everyone speaks. Give each student a handout similar to the following one, instead of asking them to do a cold reading of the chapter. Encourage students to talk through a Prereading workshop to determine what they already know about the content of the chapter. **They should make no notes, just talk.** If they can complete most of the open-ended statements and answer the questions with confidence, then they do not have to spend much time reading the chapter; if they are stumped by much of the workshop, they need to read the chapter most carefully.

*Prereading Workshop based on **Western Wind**, Chapter Two*

Below you will find open-ended statements and questions which are keys to fully understanding the chapter's content. Answer each to the best of your ability within a peer group. At this point in your reading process, don't be concerned if you draw a few blanks and have nothing to say about some of the material. Chapter 2 will clear up problems.

- I often use figurative comparisons when...
- When I am tired, I often say, "I'm as tired as a ..."
- When I'm really happy, I will often say, "This is..."
- What is a simile? Give an example of a simile.
- What is a metaphor? Give an example.
- If a poet does not use figurative comparisons, the poem will probably...
- Analogy is...
- If I were to compare myself to a literary or mythological character, it would be to...
- An allusion is...
- An example of personification in a Walt Disney film is...

Experience

When you have finished the prereading workshop,
- make a journal entry to discuss your findings. How much did you already know? On what part of the chapter should you concentrate most?
- read only the poems in the chapter. Think about them and how they have affected you.
- make a journal entry on your reactions to the poems.
- afterwards, read the entire chapter as thoroughly as you think necessary.
- make a journal entry on your comprehension of the chapter, applying your new knowledge to the poems that are in the chapter.

Preparation for Active Learning

- Breakfast with Poetic Terms (wait for a handout)
- Teach a Poem: find one poem from the anthology – pages 397ff – which contains examples of figurative comparisons. (Details will be given later.)
- Answer in your journal A, B, C, and E from pages 43-46.

Application and Synthesis

- Poetry Synthesis: Compose a new stanza for the poem that you are going to teach. Make sure that you introduce at least one example of a figurative comparison.

Hint: After providing one or two such workshops for the first chapters of the textbook, divide the class into small groups and assign each group one of the remaining chapters. It will be the responsibility of each group to provide a similar workshop for one chapter. In other words, one group of students will make up a workshop on a chapter for the rest of the students. Ask them to submit a typed copy so that you can duplicate it for the whole class. (If there are problems, or the handout is not up to your standards or expectations, you may have to ask the group to submit a new handout for duplication.)

• Examine the following Prereading workshop composed by four students:

Prereading Workshop based on *Understanding Movies*, Chapter Nine

Made up by David, Heather, Craig, and Andrew.*

Below you will find open-ended statements and questions which will help you to understand the chapter's content. Ask yourself each and answer to the best of your knowledge within a peer group. (Don't worry about not being able to answer some of them right away.)

• A documentary film is...
• How do documentaries differ from other types of films?
• When I first turn on the TV, I know I'm watching a documentary because...
• My favorite documentaries are those that...
• What distinguishes a good documentary from a mediocre one?
• Artistry is involved in documentary-making via the...
• Documentaries are studies of objectivity in film making because...
• Documentaries are studies in subjectivity in film making because...

Experience

• Before you read the chapter, study the photos in it. Examine the photos first WITHOUT READING THE CAPTIONS. Which ones are easily identifiable as documentary shots? Why? Which ones look suspiciously like scenes from avant-garde films? How can you tell?
• When you have finished prereading, make a journal entry to discuss your findings. Which parts of the chapter do you already know? Which parts are you going to have to study carefully?
• Afterwards, read Chapter Nine.
• Make a journal entry on your comprehension of the chapter. Afterwards, comment further on any of the items from your "Prereading Workshop" section that had given you trouble.

Application and Synthesis

• The next time you watch a TV documentary, apply what is in Chapter Nine to the program to help you appreciate it more.

---

* Students record their names on the handout and take over the class for the workshop. They have become the authorities on that chapter.

Hint: Remember that, after you have made up a Prereading workshop on the first two chapters of a textbook, you give the task to your students. Because they feel the responsibility of learning is on their shoulders, they will quite often surprise you with effective, new ideas to make the reading of a chapter interesting, meaningful, and even exciting.

Reading Journals

Teacher Preparation: Ask students to purchase an exercise book or other book suitable for use as a journal.
Length of Time: As homework, at least 10 minutes each day.

- Encourage students to keep a Reading Journal so that they can write their personal responses to what they read: predicting what will happen next in a story, suggesting what results a chemistry experiment might produce, making up questions to ask peers or their teacher about things they don't quite understand, etc.
- On a regular basis, you might form small groups so that students have time to discuss the content of their Reading Journals with their peers. You might have a follow-up session so that you can answer any unanswered questions.
- Students should also keep facts and details in their journals about what they read. Instead of having to waste a lot of time memorizing all of the details of a course, they should keep them in their journals for easy reference. During exams, term essays, or any kind of preparation for presentations, they should have free access to the facts and details in their journals so that they can readily apply them.
- As well as asking students to react to what they read, encourage them to react in their journals to what they see and hear. Instead of taking time to write notes during an active-learning workshop, students should take time in their journals to reflect on the workshop by including relevant details that they may want to refer to at a later date.
- Instruct students to date and even title each entry.

Hint: I give a participation mark for students. It involves their attendance and active participation in the various workshops. It also includes their journals. Twice during the term I will ask to see their journals; for example, I will say, "Show me May 2's entry." If they can't show it, they must show me May 1's or May 3's entry, since they are supposed to make six entries a week.

Ethnic Stories

Teacher Preparation: If you have a large number of students with English as a Second Language, ask them to bring texts in their native language.
Length of Time: Depends on how many ESL students you have.

- This workshop should help ESL students having difficulty with idiom. They should bring a story or a textbook chapter from their native country (already translated or one they can translate themselves). The benefits of their choosing their own stories or textbooks are many, but two are worth mentioning. First, ESL students will not have the problem of missing many allusions that educated English-speaking readers take for granted. Second, you can deal with the characteristics of stories or with the thesis of a chapter without having to explain the deeper meaning of many sections of text.
- You can repeat this workshop several times as needed.

Reading Club

Teacher Preparation: Just make an announcement.

If you find that you have a number of students who have reading difficulties, help them to start a Reading Club. Negotiate a time when they will meet: before classes begin, after school, or some other time that they may suggest.

- Every once in a while one of the students might put a notice on the chalkboard, "The Reading Club is meeting at Sharon's house at 7:30 this Saturday to talk about Chapter 8. Be on time!"
- Although I have told my students who are involved in reading clubs that I would be happy to come to any of their meetings if they are having difficulties, I've not yet been asked to attend any. I do know, however, that students are benefitting greatly from having their peers reading with them. Surprisingly, some students have told me that this is the first time they have ever finished reading a novel.

IDEAS FOR READING WORKSHOPS

CHAPTER FOUR

Writing Icebreakers

No matter the grade or subject, students usually struggle with writing. By helping students make everything they write as real and relevant as possible, teachers allow students to have a sense of ownership of their pieces of writing. Taking students through a series of writing workshops will help them enjoy the process of writing.

Informed and Uninformed Audience

Teacher Preparation: Using the following material and your own feelings about "Audience," prepare a short lecture/discussion.
Length of Time: 10 minutes.

- One of the biggest barriers students must hurdle before they begin to write is "What can I possibly write to interest my teacher? She's been teaching this course for the past 20 years and knows everything about it. So what can I say that she doesn't already know?" With thoughts like these, students are doomed to failure before they begin to write to someone they consider a highly *informed* reader.
- When students write only for a teacher and only to achieve a grade, they usually produce non-pieces of writing that have no real sense of audience. After all, where else except in school do people have their writing corrected and graded? Perhaps that is why so few students write after they leave school; their years of writing papers only to have them dissected, corrected, and graded have convinced them that what they write has little intrinsic value.
- To overcome these real problems, you should encourage students to write to other *uninformed* audiences. Then, you can become your students' editor, helping them to get their papers ready for their intended readers. Along the way, you can still assign grades, but you will be much more pleased with the papers because they will have a sense of audience.
- So, to prepare students to write for the rest of their lives, encourage them to write to an audience who really *wants* to read what they have written. If this sounds impossible, suggest they make up an audience – and even pretend to write in a different voice from their own. Implementing these ideas, students will both stretch their imaginative powers and produce unique products.
- Read the following analysis papers on James Joyce's "Araby," written by two students for an *uninformed* audience. (Note: these are excerpts, not whole papers.) As you read, note the sense of audience (and purpose) that each contains. After you finish reading each excerpt, assume that you are the students' English teacher. How would you feel receiving these papers? What would you suggest they do with their pieces to rewrite them as a formal analysis for an *informed* audience?

- If your class is familiar with "Araby," you might like to duplicate these excerpts for your students to analyze.

Writing for an Uninformed Audience

1. Dear Charlie,

 I know you have read the story "Araby," Charlie, and can't understand the plot. But James Joyce has written a story which explains the age you are at right now. The story is mainly about a boy like yourself, jumping back and forth between illusion and reality.

 Remember the crush you had on Cindy last summer? The boy in "Araby" also had a crush; not on the girl next door, but on love itself. I'm telling you the truth! Can you recall in the story the boy murmuring: "O love! O love!" and he doesn't even know her name, only that she's Mangan's sister? On top of his love with love, the boy thinks he's a knight carrying a chalice. Both you and I know the chalice is really a shopping bag. Remember, Charlie, when mom gave you the watermelon to carry home from the Safeway and you pretended it was a football, to be carried down the field (sidewalk) for seven points? Are you beginning to see how "Araby" relates to you and how the story goes from illusion to reality?...

 Glenn

2. Galahad,

 I've just finished reading James Joyce's "Araby" and can understand why you like it so much. Images of you spring to my mind immediately. Joyce's young lad's romantic notions and adventurous spirit depict a roving knight. Chivalrous, frivolous, and brave is this young man – much like you.

 Your familiar soldier-of-fortune attitude is described in the episode on a busy street where the boy "imagined that [he] bore [his] chalice safely through a throng of foes."

 He fancies a neighboring lass and I chuckle with nostalgic recollections of your past infatuations. Joyce describes this dreamy lad and states, "Every morning [he] lay on the floor...watching her door." ... He could not look directly into "love's" face but "the white curve of her neck" and "...border of her petticoat" projected an image of a damsel in waiting. Waiting for a treasure from such a magical place.

 Both of you decided to travel distances from home to obtain the prize.... I remember you telling me of that darkened evening and the blackness of the well, housing the much-awaited Holy Grail. The lad in "Araby" also gazed "up in the darkness" to see "himself as a creature driven and derided by vanity." Did you also feel this way?...

 King Arthur

- In future, try to assign writing projects that allow students to claim ownership of their products; for example, "Using one of the analysis key words [Chapter 2], write a 400-word paper on one aspect of *Macbeth* for an audience of your choice," or "Using one of the evaluation key words [Chapter 2], write a critique of Freud's Oedipus Complex for anyone but me," or "Using one of the synthesis key words [Chapter 2], produce an original product for your parents that links one piece of literature you've been reading to what we've been studying in geography."

Make Writing Real

Teacher Preparation: After reading the following material, prepare a
    lecture/workshop so that students understand and appreciate "writing
    variables."
Length of Time: One period.

- Perhaps one of the most important things you can do to improve the level of
  writing among students is to introduce them to the writing variables. The
  time you spend to make sure that your students understand the importance of
  using them for everything they write will benefit them for the rest of their
  writing lives.
- If the students use real variables (real audience, real purpose, real format,
  and so on), their writing will surely be more meaningful and interesting
  than otherwise. However, it is not always possible to use real variables, so
  students must learn how to make their writing *seem* real even when choosing
  fictitious variables.
- Calling your students together early in the term and illustrating how they
  might define their writing variables will probably clear up any problems they
  might encounter when they work on assignments. For example, you might
  show the usefulness of considering writing variables by presenting a copy of
  the following grid and asking students to predict which set of writing
  variables will probably produce the best product and to make up their own set
  of writing variables **using the same TOPIC**.

Writing Variables				
TOPIC	**AUDIENCE**	**PURPOSE**	**FORMAT**	**VOICE**
fear of dark	my teacher	to get credit for an assignment	expository paragraph	my own
fear of dark	my father	to tell him what caused my fear	letter	my own
fear of dark	my psychia-trist (imagined)	to tell her that my dreams are respons-ible for my fear of dark	detailed report	me, at six
fear of dark	?	?	?	?

- As a follow-up, duplicate the following material or adapt it to fit your needs to
  help your students choose precise writing variables. You may like to look
  over the material in Chapter 15 first.

Selecting Writing Variables

TOPIC:

- Is the topic limited enough to fit the assigned length of my piece of writing?
- Do I know enough about the topic or do I have to do more research?
- Should I brainstorm with a few peers or with my computer?
- Should I write lots more notes? Make an outline? (Determining the rest of the writing variables will help focus and limit the topic, so I may have to modify my Topic later.)

AUDIENCE:

- Which real audience might I write to: a fellow student, friend, family member, school newspaper, government official...**anyone but my teacher**?
- Which imagined audience might I write to: a movie star, a long-dead historical figure, a character from a novel, an extraterrestrial, a river, etc.? (Writing to a real or imagined AUDIENCE will make my writing strong.)
- How much does my audience already know about my topic?
- Why would my audience want to read my paper?
- As a result of my answer to the last two questions, what should I include/exclude in the content of what I write?
- How will my audience determine my word choice, sentence length, and general style?*

PURPOSE:

- What is my purpose for writing to my specific audience – to tell, to argue, to entertain, to explain, for any purpose except to obtain a high mark. (If my writing has a definite purpose I will achieve a high mark.)
- How is my purpose going to narrow my topic?

FORMAT:

- Which format best fulfils my purpose – descriptive paragraph, argumentative essay, lab report, poem, film script, comic strip, video production, rap session, and so on?**

VOICE:

- Will I use my own voice as the narrator of this piece of writing?
- Or will I choose to use a persona – Shakespeare, an endangered animal, a polluted beach, a pilgrim, or some other persona?
- In what way will my audience appreciate my choice of voice? How will my format change as a result?

LIMITED TOPIC:

- What is my limited topic?
- Is it narrow enough? If not, I will review my writing variables to make them more specific.
- As a result of my writing variables, what will my audience expect my piece to focus on?

---

* Instead of allowing students to choose their audience for every assignment, you might say, "For this assignment you must write to an examining board. However, you have free choice for the other writing variables."

** From time to time, you may insist that all students follow a particular format; for example, "For this assignment, you must write an argumentative essay, but you are free to choose all of the other writing variables."

- Before students begin to write their assignments, they may like to share their writing variables with others. Encourage discussion about the effectiveness of the choices of writing variables. This brainstorming session can help focus and refine the writing even more, thus saving students much time. Students will also quickly realize that they have not written the variables in stone; they may change them during this brainstorming session or, for that matter, at any time during their composing or even revising process.
- Ask students to write a product for which they have considered all of their writing variables. Later, you can take their products through some of the editing processes described in the next chapter.
- Read these excerpts from an introductory assignment I gave to my writing students during the first week of class. They all had to begin with the BROAD TOPIC of "Drugs/Alcohol." You might like to duplicate them for your class. See if they can determine the rest of the writing variables from reading these few excerpts.

Student Writing

1. Dear Mom and Dad,
   We used to be so happy. I wasn't frightened to come out of my room and I looked forward to dinner time. Now, I feel terrified. I love you because I know who you were before you started drinking, but now I hate you because I am scared of what you have become. I don't even know if you know who I am any more. In fact, I get excited when I have to go to school because I don't hide in a closet, waiting for you to pass out after polishing off a bottle. Alcohol has torn us apart....
   No one talks any more, and when you do it is about going to the store to buy more alcohol. I looked forward to your tucking me in at night; now, I cry myself to sleep. I hope one day the pain will go away. There is one thing in the world that I ask for: "Love me again as much as you love that bottle."

2. Attention School Board:
   As a teacher, I am extremely concerned about my students. Cocaine appears to be one of the most widely used drugs in high schools and I want something done about it. It might be a good idea to ask the students to write an essay on how cocaine affects their lives. This will enable the students who are not taking this drug to think about their addicted friends and to have second thoughts before trying it themselves. This will also allow the dependent ones to realize that they are endangering their own lives and need serious help....

3. Dear Abby:
   I would like to take this opportunity to address the often overlooked problem of drug abuse among senior citizens. I am certain that in your readership there are many children of the elderly who may not even be aware of their parents' drug dependencies. I hope that my letter will raise awareness of this crucial issue and encourage children to recognize symptoms of addiction displayed by their parents so that the latter may seek treatment.
   There are several reasons why this is an often overlooked problem:
   First, the symptoms of drug dependency are frequently mistaken by family members for signs of old age or senility. Even symptoms as common among seniors as insomnia, depression, confusion and minor injuries can be associated with a drug problem.
   Second...

⇨

4. I used to be a good-looking car. Now I've lost all my doors, tires, and I hear my engine is to be pulled out tomorrow. As a recently elected spokesvehicle for this wrecker's lot, I know, without doubt, most of us found our way here as a result of drunken drivers. Smashed, disabled, ruined beyond recognition because my driver plied himself with excessive drink, I was recently towed here behind a sympathetic truck....

Drivers, hear this: "It's time you start taking better care of us, your best friends....

5. I'm a mess. I need your help. The police have locked me up on an "impaired driving" charge, but I swear I was not drunk when they arrested me. I want you to come down and get me out, immediately. I would like to settle for just a ticket but I think the police are over-reacting and demanding a stiffer penalty.

My neighbors are to blame for this. I accidentally hit their garage doors. Big deal! At 3:00 a.m. in the morning anyone could misjudge distances....

Write an Ad

Teacher Preparation: Make up three envelopes along the lines described below.
Length of Time: 30 to 40 minutes

- Ask students to form groups of three or four. Each group picks one item from three different envelopes. Put slips of papers with specific details in each envelope.
- Envelope One contains the names of imaginary products — for example, Fuzzy Fun, Dad's Delight, Mother's Love, Ideal Date, Gorgeous Hunk, Pearly Dew, Pretty Patti, Wilma's Way, Macho Muncho.
- Envelope Two contains magazine or newspaper titles — *Financial Post*, *Good Housekeeping*, *Playboy*, *Weight Watchers*, *Field and Stream*, *Playgirl*, *The Catholic Digest*, *Time*, *Better Homes and Gardens*.
- Envelope Three contains the names of holidays — Valentine's Day, Labor Day, Father's Day, Christmas, New Year's Day, Easter, Mother's Day, St. Patrick's Day, Hallowe'en.
- The groups must decide what type of product would be appropriate for the audience of their chosen magazine. They must determine what kind of audience (age, sex, education, social level, etc.) would read the magazine.
- They must choose an appropriate product that fits the name — this can be anything from perfume to an Alpine resort, dog food, candy, furniture, WHATEVER.
- Then they must write an advertisement to appear in the magazine for the holiday occasion. They must consider the audience and the style of the magazine. They can use the blackboard, a large sheet of newspaper, or an overhead transparency.
- Have each group present its ad. One person reads the ad aloud, then the class guesses the magazine, occasion, and product. Then they evaluate it according to its appropriateness for its audience, its effectiveness in fulfilling its purpose (to sell, persuade, convince, buy, etc.), and its originality.

Writing Variables Across the Curriculum

Teacher and Classroom Preparation: None required.
Length of Time: 15 minutes.

- Ask students to "plan" to write five products all on the same TOPIC, for five (more or fewer is fine) of the courses they are taking. If you like, you might have your entire class reach a consensus on **one** topic so that everyone has to use the same topic. Once they have chosen their topic and the five courses, they should write a statement indicating which writing variables they consider important. For example, see what one college student came up with for the topic, "Babies." You might like to duplicate it for distribution.

Writing Variable Statements

Psychology   A research paper that illustrates "What would a male child of six be like if he were raised by apes from the time he was a baby?" After reading *Tarzan: Lord of the Apes*, I decided to investigate the possible results of such an experiment. My psychology professor has required that we write to our fellow class members.

Sociology   A term paper to point out the effects of the baby boom in our state on the educational facilities, with suggestions to the Board of Education about what it should do to prepare for the children's proper education.

Nursing   An informative essay intended to prove that a fetus aborted at twelve weeks has the same number of cells as a full-term baby. I will write to members of pro-choice organizations.

Art History   A slide show with commentary analyzing the main characteristics of artists' treatment of babies in early Renaissance paintings. My professor is an authority on this period, so I will have to do thorough research, as well as offer my own detailed observations.

English   A ballad to tell the story of the "baby" hero from the movie *Baby*. Since "Baby" is a dinosaur and the movie appeals to children, I'm going to write this ballad for children.

- As a follow-up, ask students to share their statements of writing variables with you and (if time allows) present a few to the whole class.

Writing Folders

Teacher Preparation: Just make an announcement. For younger grades you may like to take class time to show students how to construct (and decorate) a writing folder.

- A writing folder is a resource for writing. It should contain three major parts: one for the ideas, brainstorming notes, and exploratory materials to help students compose (see Chapter 8); a second for drafts of work in progress (see the next chapter); and a third for copies of finished work.

- Students can easily make writing folders out of file folders. Let them design their own.
- During an editing session, both editor and writer can refer to the contents of a writing folder to solve difficulties or discover new material.

Invisible Writing

Teacher Preparation: None required.
Student Preparation: Students will need a pen that has run out of ink and two pieces of paper and a sheet of carbon paper. Or, if they are working on a computer, they should darken the screen.
Length of Time: Never more than 10 minutes.

- If your students get "hung up" on writing because they are always trying to "get it right" the first time, engage them in Invisible Writing.
- Have students insert the carbon paper between the two blank sheets, then write with the broken pen so that they can't see what they're writing. Students at a terminal would keep the screen dark for the full ten minutes.
- Writing invisibly forces students to carry on to the end of their writing project instead of looking back, changing wording, or correcting errors. When they finish an Invisible Writing session, they should read the carbon copy, or turn on the screen, and read what they've written. Ask them, "What do you think of what you wrote? Have you developed your idea? Does your piece need much editing? Do you notice any errors?"
- You can ask students to revise what they wrote, or just move on to another project.

Collaborative Writing

Teacher Preparation: Adapt the material below to fit your needs and prepare a handout of instructions for collaborative writing.
Length of Time: From the introduction of this project to its completion will take two weeks; sometimes students will work together in class and sometimes on their own at home.

- If you have a number of poor or reluctant writers in the room, you might like to divide the class into groups of four and have each group produce a single essay. By introducing this writing project early in the term, you will ensure that students learn to develop their writing process so that when they have to do an essay on their own, they quite naturally follow a similar process approach.
- Have groups appoint a leader who will be the liaison between you and the group, organize discussion to ensure that everyone in the group gets a chance to talk, and make up a timetable so that the members of the group complete their tasks on time. The leader will make sure that the group meets all deadlines.
- To make the assignment more real, you might have each group make up a series of topics that they would like to work on. All groups should give their lists of topics to the group to their right. That group should choose *one* of the topics and ask the first group to write to them. Each group, therefore, will be writing to four of their classmates.

Hint: To make collaborative writing work well, have students work on an informative essay rather than an argumentative paper. Collaborative writing helps students focus on structuring an essay: thesis statements, methods of organization, use of research material, mechanics, etc. They should not have to all agree on a single issue and take a firm stand in order to argue from one point of view.

- The students in each group must determine whether they have enough information to begin to write. If not, they should do the necessary research: one researching books; another, periodicals; another, newspapers; and another, interviewing. They should then have a session to pool their information.
- They should construct several thesis statements and choose the one they think will work best for them. You might insist on approving their chosen thesis statement *before* they begin to draft their essay. Collaborative writing is designed to help all students to improve their standard of writing, so they should concentrate more on quality than quantity.
- Once you have accepted the thesis statement, students should first compose a full set of writing variables. Then they should decide on a method of organization and a style. Are they going to compare and contrast, set up a cause/effect organization, organize chronologically, sequentially, climactically, or employ another method of organization?
- During their writing process, expect to be invited (or invite yourself) to visit groups to assist them with particular problems: organization, setting up a bibliography, clarification, etc.
- Then, they should divide the duties of writing the essay: three members could be responsible for the body, the fourth for the introduction and conclusion. On a day designated by the leader, they should bring their work to a group meeting and, as a group, pull the essay together so that it has a consistent development and style. When they have completed the first draft, they should self-edit and revise. They should then give their next draft to another peer group (not the group who is their intended audience) to edit.
- After having the essay peer-edited, the group leader should make a half-hour appointment, during class time (or another convenient time), so that you can conduct a 4-to-1 conference. (Make sure that the leader provides one copy of the essay for you and one for each of the writers.) During this conference, you can provide suggestions and comments and, if you wish, a grade as well.

Hint: I usually read the essay aloud while they follow along. They can hear when I have difficulties and can discuss ways to revise. Students will also be able to write their impressions of your suggestions on their own copies and, if you require a rewrite, be able to offer specific details to the group when they meet again to discuss rewriting the essay.

- Without doubt, students learn a great deal more from the 4-to-1 conferencing approach than they would if you were to take home the papers and hand them back graded. Using this method, you will have only one quarter of the usual number of essays to mark, since each member of the group will receive the same mark for the essay.
- Finally, after they have written their final draft, they should give their essay to their intended audience.
- As a follow-up to collaborative writing, you might ask each group to write a letter of appreciation to the writers, indicating what they liked best about the essay. Keep the letter positive. (If you wish to grade the assignment, have the leaders submit a copy of the essay and letter to you.)

Writing Journal

Teacher Preparation: Ask students to keep a Writing Journal.
Student Preparation: Students should purchase a bound exercise book or a
   bound, hardcover book that has blank pages.
Length of Time: 10 minutes a day.

- Keeping a writing journal is one way for students to discover that they have
  many interesting, valuable thoughts and experiences to record. They can
  also make their journal a storehouse of information from their reading
  projects (see "Reading Journal" in the preceding chapter).
- Duplicate or adapt the following Question/Answer information sheet about
  journal writing.

Journal Writing

What is a journal? A book in which you write about your feelings, thoughts, and
experiences. Or about your school work.

Who will read my journal? Only you. Or anyone to whom you care to show it.

What is the point of writing in a journal? To get in touch with yourself or your
school work. If you date and title each journal entry, you can refer to it easily.

Why is it necessary to write in my journal every day? Your goal should be to
create a habit of writing. Instead of having to take copious notes during classes,
you can sit comfortably at home and write about what happened during the day.

May I use any of my journal writing for other assignments? Certainly. You
might be able to find the exact bit of information you need to include in a term
paper, midterm, or final exam.

What do I do with my journal at the end of the school term? That is up to you. If
you have begun the habit of journal writing, you will probably keep it up long
after term's end.

Take A Walk to Brainstorm

- By encouraging students to walk in pairs to help brainstorm an idea for an
  essay draft, you help solidify the classroom learning community. While
  walking, students feel less threatened; the topic under discussion becomes
  more real.
- From time to time you might ask your students to Take A Walk, following
  one of the suggestions below. Later, you will probably invent several relevant
  reasons for your students to take further walks.
- If, for any number of reasons, you wish to have students always within
  earshot, you might set boundaries for their walk. If students are not allowed
  to go outside your classroom, you can still have them participate in these
  workshops – instead of walking, they will just chat. The point is that they
  give each other undivided attention; therefore, they concentrate solely on
  what their companion says.

Discussion Walk

Teacher and Classroom Preparation: Think of relevant discussion topics.
    Give a quotation, poem, short story, or chapter to the class.
Length of Time: 15 minutes.

- After they have read the material, ask them to take a 10-minute walk to discuss their impressions. When they return, they should look at the text and discuss specific points for five more minutes.

Walk to Brainstorm

Teacher and Classroom Preparation: None required.
Length of Time: 15 minutes.

- As a brainstorming technique, a pair of students can go for a 15-minute walk to discuss their thoughts on a particular topic. Their task is to focus and limit the topic to the point where they are able to begin their first draft. Students should focus their attention on one topic per walk; therefore, both the writer and his/her partner should brainstorm only that topic.

Consider Walking! Instead of sitting at desks in a classroom, students are more likely to brainstorm better while walking about their campus. You can easily put many of the workshops in this book "on their feet" and take them out of the classroom for better results. Why not ask the students to Take A Walk during the Pro/Con (Chapter 9) or the Biog Talk (Chapter 1) workshops?

Frequent Writers Club

Teacher Preparation: Just make an announcement.

- If you have students who are eager to improve their writing skills, you probably don't have enough class time to provide encouragement and opportunity for them to share their work with other keen writers and readers. So why not suggest that these students form a Frequent Writers Club, which would arrange to meet regularly after school or on weekends?
- You might like to be present during the first meeting of the Frequent Writers Club, to help get it off and running. During this meeting, establish the following objectives, no matter the subject or grade level of the students:
    - Set your own goals — for example, you each might like to produce a piece of writing every three weeks or so.
    - Generally, topics of your papers should be related to course content, although you may wish to synthesize material from two or more courses.
    - Don't limit yourselves to a particular format or number of words.
    - At the next meeting, share your pieces and invite evaluation. Because the Club is for people who like to write and want to improve their writing style, you should not bring "required" assignments to the meetings. Setting your own topics and evaluating your work within the Club will ensure that you maintain ownership of your writing and not concern yourself with writing for marks.

- After the first meeting, encourage students to appoint a chair who can occasionally report to you on the progress of the Club.
- The Frequent Writers Club can give students in English, math, science — in fact, students in all subjects — the chance to produce many creative pieces.

Apprehensive Writers

Teacher Preparation: Read over the following information and prepare accordingly.

- Some students lack confidence in their writing ability and find it especially hard to write a "demand essay." If you suspect one or more of your students of being anxious about writing, you might like to give them the following questionnaire to find out more about their attitudes:

Test Your Attitude Toward Writing

Beside each statement, write "Never," "Sometimes," or "Always."

1. I will do anything rather than write.
2. I like to write as long as no one reads what I've written.
3. I am afraid of writing.
4. When I must produce an essay, my biggest problem is which of my many good ideas I should write about.
5. When I sit down to write, my mind is usually as empty as the blank page I'm staring at.
6. I know I express myself clearly when I write.
7. When I give people something I have written, they usually say they like it.
8. I like to write
9. I don't have to hand in an essay to find out it's bad; I already know I've done a poor job.
10. It's easy for me to write a good composition.
11. If I can, I always show my friends what I write before I hand it in to be graded.
12. I like to have my writing evaluated.
13. I am proud of what I write.
14. I keep changing everything I write; I am never satisfied with what I produce.
15. I keep a copy of nearly everything I write because I am proud of it or may need it for future reference.

- Give your apprehensive writers (or your whole class) these lists of characteristics of good and poor writers. Then ask them to respond to the four questions after the lists.

Good Writers

- concentrate on generating ideas
- experiment by writing several drafts
- do not allow small errors to interfere with their writing process
- revise or even discard while they write
- are not afraid to take chances
- follow their instincts
- learn from their mistakes
- keep their audience in mind
- are always aware of why they are writing

Poor Writers

- write as quickly as possible
- do not use any exploring or prewriting activities
- will try to salvage a piece of writing (even if they know it is inadequate) rather than throw it away and start again
- get locked into completing a sentence because they do not want to admit they made a mistake
- try to get everything right the first time, stopping the flow of ideas to check the correctness of spelling, punctuation, and grammar
- do not reread their papers, let alone revise or rewrite them; seldom revise sentence structure to make what they say more emphatic
- believe quantity is more important than quality (papers from poor writings are often longer than those from good writers)
- write to no one in particular

1. Which characteristics from the above lists apply to you?
2. Which ones have never applied to you?
3. Which ones will you try to incorporate into your writing process? How will you do so?
4. Which ones will you not be able to incorporate into your writing process? Why?

Writing about Life

Teacher Preparation: From time to time – no matter the course content – you might like to present your class with a profound, stimulating quotation similar to the ones below.

Length of Time: 15 minutes.

- "Education is not the purpose of life; education is life itself." If you agree, from time to time encourage students to think about how their lives are changed because they find themselves in your science, math, English, or history class. You and they might find the exercise refreshing and enlightening.
- So, once every four weeks, you might ask your students to write non-stop to link the content of a quotation with the content of your course and with their own lives.

- If you like, after the students have completed their pieces, you could use the rest of the period to have them share their work with others. (See Chapter 5 for editing ideas.) If time presses on and you *must* get back to the course curriculum, you may choose not to evaluate the pieces; however, asking your students to Write about Life for 15 minutes lets them know that you think writing is important.
- Here are a few quotations to get you started:

> The earth is precious. It was not given to you by your parents. It was loaned to you by your children. (Kenyan mythology)

> Follow your bliss. (Joseph Campbell)

> Birth is a moment of transcendence which we spend our lives trying to understand. (Salman Rushdie)

> Our antagonist is our helper. (Edmund Burke) Ever tried. Ever failed. Never mind. Try again. Fail better. (Samuel Beckett)

YOUR OWN WRITING ICEBREAKERS

CHAPTER FIVE

Peer-Editing Icebreakers

Most teachers would agree that students find writing the most difficult form of communication. They would also agree that many students find peer-editing even more difficult.

Professional writers know that writing is permanent. Once a piece is published, it can be reread, analyzed, evaluated. Professional writers know the importance of editors and strive to make sure their published work can stand rigorous examination.

Student writers, on the other hand, often submit work that has not been edited by anyone – including the writers themselves. They are used to simply submitting their written assignments and having them returned with marginal comments and a fixed grade. They are even used to reading the same comments repeated over and over on subsequent papers. Invariably, they do not understand the meaning of terms such as AWK, VAGUE, UNCLEAR, COMMA SPLICE, AGREEMENT PROBLEMS, CONFUSING, let alone how to correct their writing to eliminate the problems.

Before you mark your next set of papers, ask your students to tell you *exactly* what they think UNCLEAR or AWK means and exactly how they would rewrite to get rid of these problems.

Some facts about grading student papers:

- Simply marking and returning papers with comments and grades, teachers can expect approximately a 2% improvement in their students' standard of writing. All that red ink for a 2% improvement!
- Many papers do not warrant the time and effort teachers put into them.
- A peer-editing session weeds out many errors before papers reach the teacher's eyes, and if students know what makes a good paper before they edit (and before they start to compose), assignments improve dramatically.
- A one-to-one tutorial session with a teacher helps student writers more than any other form of editing. And if the student has a sense of controlling the session, with the opportunity to ask questions instead of having to answer them or defend a paper, more improvement occurs.
- Inviting the peer editor to be present during a tutorial session will help get the attention off the writer and onto the peer editor. The results will improve both student writing and student editing.
- Teachers dedicated to active learning build into their programs times for one-to-one or small-groups-to-one tutorial sessions *within* class time. Students see their teachers at least once every two weeks *during class time*, while the rest of the class is involved in various active-learning workshops which do not need the teacher's full attention.
- So that students know exactly how you evaluate their work, you might have them build up a set of guidelines with you. Or you might like to duplicate the following guides and present them to the class so that they know what makes a paper superior, average, or unsatisfactory. They should use these guidelines when self-editing and peer-editing, and witness you using them during the conferencing sessions. Have them go over the guidelines within small groups so that they can talk about each point, asking for clarification when necessary.

How to Use the Checklists

Answer each question "Yes" or "No." If you, your peer-editors, or your teacher-editor answer "Yes" to all questions in the "Superior" section of each "Checklist," you need not go on to the "Average" questions. However, if you do not receive a "Yes" to each question, you should move down to the "Average" questions. Finally, if you do not receive an unqualified "Yes" to each question in the "Average" section, you should move down to the "Unsatisfactory" section. When you receive a "Yes" in this section, you must make some major revisions.

Content Checklist

For most nonfiction, and some fiction as well, content involves the limited topic (subject, main idea, thesis) and its development.

Superior
- Is the central idea fresh, true, specific, and clear? Is it expressed accurately and interestingly in a thesis statement or topic sentence?
- Is the idea suitable for the length of the work and is it well developed?
- Is the central idea supported with high-quality facts, reasons, examples, or other concrete details?

Average
- Is the thesis statement or topic sentence clear but not very interesting or original?
- Does the development rely on predictable details?
- Is the development incomplete or repetitious and does it include unimportant, obvious, or occasionally unrelated facts?
- Is the limited topic logically developed?

Unsatisfactory
- Is there no central idea, or is the central idea not clearly expressed in a thesis statement or topic sentence? If it is clearly expressed, is the central idea dull or unimportant?
- If there is a good idea, is it supported by inappropriate details?
- Is the development of the main idea confused?
- Are the thesis statement and its development inappropriate for the length of the project so that the idea is either underdeveloped or repeated?

How would you judge the content of the piece of writing: superior, average, or unsatisfactory? Why?

Organization Checklist

Organization involves how a piece of writing is developed, how the sentences within a paragraph are linked, and how the writing moves from one sentence or paragraph to the next.

Superior
- Is the central idea developed clearly and logically? Have the writing variables been taken into account? Can the audience move effortlessly from one section of the work to the next?
- Has the writing been specifically organized; for example, has it been organized with comparisons, causes and effects, spatial, chronological or climactic order, and so on? Has each supporting detail just the right emphasis? Are the supporting details in exactly the right places in the work?
- Does everything in the work belong?

Average
- Does the writing seem to have an organizational plan, but at times lose its focus?
- Is there something wrong with the emphasis or order of some of the points? Are they stressed too much or not enough, or are they in the wrong place?
- Is the writing sometimes hard to follow because there are not sufficient transitional devices to move the audience from one point to the next?
- Are there too many transitional words so that the writing talks down to the audience?

Unsatisfactory
- Is there no clear organization?
- Are the supporting details either incomplete or repetitive?
- Are the paragraphs not unified or incoherent because there are either insufficient or confusing transitions?
- Has a new idea been introduced into a paragraph before a previous idea has been fully developed?

How would you judge the organization of the piece of writing: superior, average, or unsatisfactory? Why?

Style Checklist

Style involves not only the choice of particular words and sentences but also their effectiveness, arrangement, and appropriateness.

Superior
- Does the audience always stay on track because the point of view (focus) is the same throughout the piece?
- Are the sentences of different lengths and types? Are the thoughts expressed in interesting ways?
- Is the word choice clear and accurate?
- Has the level of language stayed the same throughout?
- Does the writing contain effective figurative language such as analogies, metaphors, or similes?
- Do the beginning and ending of the piece seem just right?

Average
- Is the sentence structure correct but unexciting? Do sentences lack variety and emphasis? Are some sentences wordy?
- Is the language often generalized rather than specific? Are the words correct but not always clear and concise?
- Are levels of language sometimes mixed?
- If figurative comparisons are used, do they sometimes not work well? Are they strained, ineffective, or inappropriate?

Unsatisfactory
- Are sentences confusing and dull?
- Do the sentences lack emphasis because of weak verbs and overused pronouns such as *it*, *this*, and *which*?
- Are the same words used over and over, or is the word choice unsuited to the purpose and intended audience?
- Does the piece contain slang, jargon, and clichés?
- Does the point of view shift constantly?
- Do idiom errors abound?

How would you judge the style of the piece of writing: superior, average, or unsatisfactory? Why?

Usage and Mechanics Checklist

Usage and mechanics deal with the nitty-gritty of writing: spelling, punctuation, grammar, and so on.

Superior
- Are grammar, punctuation, and spelling generally accurate?
- Is the writing almost free of small mechanical errors such as misuse of apostrophes and hyphens, errors in citing numbers or in using capital letters, and so on?
- Is the writing correctly punctuated? Does the piece contain more complex punctuation marks, such as semicolons, parentheses, and dashes, as well as double and single quotation marks if appropriate?
- Is the writing free of serious sentence errors, such as fragment faults, dangling modifiers, run-on sentences, and so on?

Average
- Do occasional mechanical errors creep into the writing?
- Does the writing, though correct and careful, contain only commas and periods when semicolons, colons, and dashes might be more appropriate?

Unsatisfactory
- Because of mechanical errors, will the audience often not understand the writing; for example, do tenses or voices shift in mid-sentence, sentences run together, or unintentional sentence fragments try to stand as complete thoughts?
- Are punctuation marks missing or incorrectly used?
- Are there frequent spelling errors?
- Are many pronoun references unclear?
- Does the writing contain incorrect or inappropriate word choices?
- Are recognized idioms fractured?

How would you judge the usage and mechanics in the piece of writing: superior, average, or unsatisfactory? Why?

The Benefits of Peer Editing

Many scholars have written about peer editing; most sing its praises, knowing that peer editing is beneficial to both writers and editors. We have all seen the power of peer pressure. If we can harness it in the classroom so that students exert pressure to improve writing, not only in English classes but across the curriculum, we will surely raise levels of writing.

However, as long as teachers in other subject areas leave the responsibility for helping students improve their writing to teachers of English, the standards of writing will remain low. Some teachers of other subjects have come to realize the importance of encouraging their students to write at every opportunity. For example, math teachers of my acquaintance assign, from time to time, a piece of writing in which students must explain how they perform a mathematical equation. They let students know that writing is important.

To break students into peer editing gently, try the following workshops:

Circle Editing

Teacher Preparation: Ask students to bring a finished piece of writing to class, which they have prepared by double spacing and leaving a margin on the right and left sides of each page, leaving plenty of room for editorial comments. They should also number each sentence and place a circle around the number. Students who wish anonymity can use a three-digit number on their essays instead of their names.

Classroom Preparation: Arrange desks in a circle – the larger the circle, the better. Place a completed assignment on each desk.

Length of Time: 30 minutes.

- Ask students to read the assignment in front of them and comment on its general appearance. "Does it look inviting to read? Is it legible?" Ask them to write their impressions in pencil on the paper and pass it to the right. Then ask students to read the entire paper and comment on what they learned from reading the paper: "If the paper is a literary essay, do you appreciate the original story more, now that you've read this essay? If you'd like to thank the writer for giving you a better insight into the topic, do so. If you didn't learn anything from the essay, say so."

  Then have them pass the paper to the right. Now ask for a comment on the title of the paper they've just received: "Does it make you want to read the assignment? Is it dull? Does it catch your attention? It should not be underlined or have quotation marks around it." Ask them to write their response near the title.

- Then pass the paper to the right. Each time the paper passes, ask another question. Although you will soon gather a long list of questions appropriate to various assignments, here is a partial list I use for a literary essay (make up your own list for other formats):

    - Quickly read the paper that you've just received. Make a statement about its organization. Do you see a specific method of organization – chronological, sequential, climactic, comparison/contrast, etc.? If you do not, make a comment.
    - Circle all transitional devices. Make a comment on their effectiveness. Or suggest some specific transitional devices you think will work well.
    - Has the writer told too much plot? If so, suggest cuts. Plot information should be used only to support the thesis.
    - Find the thesis and underline all support for it. If you find a sentence that does not support the thesis, suggest that the writer omit the sentence.
    - Does the conclusion satisfy you? If not, say so. Make a suggestion to help the conclusion.
    - Draw a box around the sentence you like best. Say why.
    - Draw a circle around the sentence you dislike most. Say why.
    - After reading the assignment, comment on its worth. What mark would you give it? Why? If the writer takes into account all of the editorial comments that other editors have shared, what mark do you think the piece would receive?

Hint: In order to comment on the above suggestions, students need to read all or most of the essay each time the paper comes to them; to deal with the following suggestions, students only need to focus on small parts of the essay.

    - Are the title and author of the work the essay discusses mentioned in the first or second sentence?

— If the work is a short story, does the title have quotation marks around it rather than being underlined? If a comma or period follows the title, do the quotation marks follow the comma or period (," or .")?

— How many times has the writer used direct quotations from the work? Write the number of times at the end of the essay. Is the end punctuation correct? Remember, a comma or period comes **before** closing quotation marks; a semicolon or colon comes **after**. And exclamation points and question marks can come before or after, depending on whether they are part of the quotation or part of the writer's prose.

— Has the writer consistently used third-person point of view? Check to see if *I, me, my, we, us,* or *you* appears.

— Has the writer consistently used present tense? If past tense appears, suggest a change. If past tense appears in a quotation, suggest that the writer change it to present tense within brackets [ ].

— At the end of the essay, copy down the first three words of each sentence. Make a comment on word choice. Should there be more variety? Is there already lots of variety?

— Underline each verb. Make a list of all weak verbs (*is, are, seems, gets,* etc.) and all repetitions. Make a comment if you think the writer should work on verb choice.

— Put a square around each use of *it, that,* and *this.* Can you determine the antecedent of each? If not, say so. Suggest that the writer use a specific noun instead of a weak pronoun.

— Check for any spelling errors. Even if you only suspect that a word is misspelled, place "sp" above it. Include missing or misplaced apostrophes and hyphens as spelling errors. The writer can later check to see if there is an error.

Hint: If you wish students to make editorial suggestions, ask "Has anyone a suggestion for us all to consider?" Since students are doing the editing, they may see problems that you don't.

• Because each student only has to focus on one thing at a time, circle editing is a good icebreaker. It's painless and non-threatening.

• When the workshop ends, writers will find comments, most of them useful, written all over their papers. They can use the comments to revise their papers. Later, they might have a peer-editing session with one other student. Finally, they might have a one-to-one tutorial with the teacher. (See "One-to-One Plus One" below.)

Double Circle Editing

Teacher Preparation and Length of Time: Same as Circle Editing.

Classroom Preparation: If your space is too small for a single circle, use Double Circles. This workshop works similarly to Circle Editing, but you form two circles: an inner and outer circle. The inner circle faces out; the outer faces in.

• Start by having students from both circles handing their papers to someone in the other circle. From then on they pass their papers to the right, and proceed according to the above instructions.

Trio Editing

Teacher and Classroom Preparation: On a day when a short piece of writing is due, form peer groups of three. Sometimes I stand at the door and assign groups. first three that enter form a group, next three another group, and so on.

Length of Time: 20 minutes.

* Basically, the task of the trio of writers is to find the best piece and edit it for presentation to the rest of the class. The entire editing process stops at the end of 20 minutes, once all of the students have presented the best from each group. As a variation, you might ask the peer groups to choose the one that works least well and to bring it up to presentation standards.
* Students should spend five minutes reading their own pieces to the others in their group. Then they should choose the piece they will present to the rest of the class.
* For ten minutes they should edit the piece, readying it for oral presentation.
* For five minutes, one member from each group should read the piece aloud to the rest of the class for enjoyment and evaluation.

Hint: If students have not done the assignment, do not let them participate in the workshop. They should form a group which you can visit to find out why they didn't do the assignment. While the other groups are editing, the "delinquent" group (who are sitting at the front) are working on the assignment. Generally, students do not like to be singled out and forced to be part of the "delinquent" group, so they come with their next assignment completed. By not allowing unprepared students to participate, you help those students who are prepared to get on with their work instead of having to cover for their peers.

Find the Best

Teacher and Classroom Preparation: This workshop works well if everyone works on the same assignment and saves your having to mark stacks of papers on the same topic. Have students use a three-digit number instead of their names.

Length of Time: One full period.

* When students arrive, collect all the assignments. Have students form small groups (three or four in each group). Give a selection of assignments to each group with these instructions:
  - Take turns reading each piece of writing aloud.
  - Determine which one works best.
  - Record the number of the one you think works best
  - Pass all the papers to the group to your right.
  - When you receive the next batch of papers, repeat the above four instructions.
* When all groups have read and reacted to all papers, record the "best" papers on the chalkboard by writing down the three-digit numbers. Students might be surprised to see the same number appearing several times because several groups found that the same paper worked best. Select two or three of the best papers. You can either have the writers read their own papers to the class or you can read them. Have a follow-up discussion to determine why these papers were considered the best. In this way, the class is building up a list of criteria for what makes a good piece of writing.

Hint: Use this workshop for analysis topics such as "Point out why Oedipus gouges out his eyes." "What were the major causes of World War One?" "Identify the best methods for dealing with an oil spill in the open ocean." "Identify Galileo's contributions to the development of modern science."

Take A Walk to Edit

* Run the following editing workshops as described in "Take-A-Walk to Brainstorm" in the previous chapter.

"Karate Kid" Walk

Teacher and Classroom Preparation: After you have marked an assignment, essay exam, midterm, or any other piece of writing (or any type of exam or quiz), arrange the papers from the highest mark to the lowest mark. Whenever possible, I arrange the desks so that I have only two long, snaking rows. Place the paper with the highest mark on the first desk in a row; place the paper with the lowest mark on the desk beside it. Then, on the next pair of desks, place the papers with the next highest and next lowest marks. So that you will not end with pairs of papers receiving virtually the same marks, do a little juggling of papers. But do put the best papers with the worst for the first half of your class. THERE IS NO NEED TO TELL THE STUDENTS THAT THE FIRST ROW CONTAINS ALL THE BETTER STUDENTS AND THE SECOND ALL THE POORER STUDENTS.
Length of Time: 20 minutes.

* When students enter the room, ask them to find their paper and sit at that desk. Ask them to exchange papers with the person beside them. Then ask them to read the papers with great care in order to prepare for a 10-minute walk. (They will not be able to take the paper with them on the walk.) After five minutes, or when everyone has finished reading, tell them that they are going on a "Karate Kid" Walk. To help them prepare, say to the first row (the better students), "You are to assume the role of the wise Teacher, a *sensei*." To the second row, "You are to assume the role of the eager-to-learn Student." Then continue, "Teachers, you are to help your Students learn how to write a better _____ (exam, essay, midterm). During your walk, point out as many suggestions of ways your student might improve as you can think of. Students, ask as many questions as you want. Keep up the roleplaying even though some of the 'teachers' may have received nearly the same grades as your students." Continue, "You are to walk during the entire ten minutes. No sitting or standing around. Come back in exactly ten minutes, *sensei*, with your faithful pupils!"
* If there's a student without a partner, you should take that student for a walk. In ten minutes you will be able to give so much advice to that student that he/she will approach the next piece of writing with great confidence. Probably, though, the other *sensei* will have more impact on their students than you will. The "Karate Kid" Walk clearly demonstrates peer power.
* When they return from their walk, the *sensei* should take 5 minutes to point out a few specifics by referring to their students' assignments. Some students may want to look over the *sensei's* papers again to see "how it should be done."

- Both *sensei* and students benefit from the "Karate Kid" Walk. By focusing on their students' papers, the *sensei* often discover ways to make their own papers even better. Often *sensei* will give advice to their students that they themselves have not followed. The majority of the students will benefit greatly and will doubtless approach the next assignment, exam, or whatever with confidence.
- As a follow-up, I occasionally ask the "students" a few questions. For example, "How many of you learned a lot? How many learned very little? How many feel that you will do better next time?" I also ask the *sensei* questions: "How many enjoyed helping your student? How many learned something new? How many feel that you will do a better job next time?" Invariably, most of the members of the learning community find this workshop both enjoyable and helpful.

Walk-to-Revise

Teacher and Classroom Preparation: None required, except that students must come with a completed assignment.
Length of Time: 25 minutes.

- Before students have to submit a term paper or other major assignment, ask students to bring in their final drafts for a Walk-to-Revise Workshop. They must come with their essay in as near-perfect condition as they can make it.
- When the first two students enter, they exchange essays and immediately read them in order to prepare for a fifteen-minute walk. If a student does not bring an essay, he or she simply does not participate. Students will soon see the benefits of this workshop and will not again come empty-handed.
- When students have finished reading each other's essays, give them the following instructions: "Decide whose paper you will discuss first. You will go for a fifteen-minute walk and talk about that paper and how you might revise it to make it better. Do not take the essay with you; instead, use this handout to help you focus your talk. [Give students the handout on the next page, or make up one to fit your own needs and the dictates of the assignment.] Do not sit or stand around. You may walk around the halls or the grounds of the campus. Be back in exactly 15 minutes."
- When students return, ask them to look at specific parts of the essay and talk about ways to revise them.
- After a few minutes, they should go on another fifteen-minute walk to talk about the other essay.
- As a result of their Walk-to-Revise Workshop, students will be able to reform, remold, and rewrite their essay with a greater sense of determination.
- Duplicate or adapt the following guidelines:

A Guide to the Walk-to-Revise Workshop

You as an editor can use the following points to guide your conversation with the writer. Make suggestions to the writer by saying:

- "Why not try...?"
- "Have you ever thought about...?"
- "I don't know, but I think you might try...."
- "What did you mean when you wrote...?"
- "Would you consider...?"
- "How about...?"
- "I don't know whether _____ is right or not, but if I were you, I'd check it."
- "I think that you may have some spelling errors. When we get back, let's check some of your words."
- "Are you really confident about your punctuation? I'd like you to read a few bits out loud to me because I had difficulty following your ideas."

Here are a few statements that you want to be able to say:

- I think your title is great! Not only is it totally appropriate, it also caught my attention.
- A great opening! You caught my attention. I wanted to continue reading.
- You have stated your thesis clearly. After reading it, I knew exactly what you were going to develop in your essay.
- Your thesis is quite original.
- You have included loads of support for your thesis. I'm quite convinced that your reader will be unable to think of additional support that you forgot.
- You have blended in all of the textual support with your own prose so well that I could only tell which was which because of the quotation marks.
- Your parenthetical citations and bibliography (if appropriate) were entirely accurate. All punctuation and spacing were correct.
- You don't have any two- or three-sentence paragraphs. Each developing paragraph contains different aspects of your thesis and each contains plenty of supporting evidence.
- Your method of organization is quite obvious. You have no sentences or ideas that are irrelevant. Each part of your essay links logically to the next part: one sentence flows into the next sentence; one paragraph flows into the next.
- Your conclusion is absolutely great! The wording was just right.
- Your writing style is exciting to read. I was able to read helplessly, enjoying both what you said and the way you said it.
- You have made no grammatical errors.
- You used a great sampling of punctuation marks and used them all correctly.
- Your spelling is impeccable!

Teacher Marking

Read this short passage by a frightened writer:

> English teachers have been know to put the fear of death into a beginning writer. They may say gravely, "Your writing is suffering from ambiguity," or they may nod in agreement and in unison whisper, "Redundancy!" You take your dying paper home and try to save it from a disease you have never heard of. After hours of writing, you think that you have revived it, so you submit your paper for a second opinion. When you see it a week later, you barely recognize it. Red blotches cover its poor body. There is a huge "V" in its midsection; "ROS" on every long sentence; and "AWK" scattered over its margins. You limp home, wondering if you can ever revive your bloodied piece of writing.

If you are tired of writing the same comments on students' assignments month after month, you might try to actively engage your students in conferences.

One-to-One Plus One

Teacher and Classroom Preparation: Have three desks available, one for you, one for the writer, one for the peer-editor.
Length of Time: Anywhere from 1 to 10 minutes per paper.

- Keeping a portion of each period available for teacher editing, you can easily see each of your students every other week in class time. The five to ten minutes you spend going over a student's writing with a peer editor present will improve writing standards more than taking the paper home to mark.
- As you read a paper aloud, the student writer will be able to see your delights and concerns. You may stop occasionally to ask questions or receive clarifications, asking the peer editor to explain something that you don't comprehend. You act as an ideal editor, intent on getting the paper ready for its intended audience.
- If you feel the paper is ready, say so unhesitatingly. Don't put a grade on it unless you absolutely have to. Grades interfere with the writing process, so resist grading for as long as possible.
- If a piece of writing is not ready for its audience, say so. And expect the peer editor to re-edit it before you engage in another conference. Don't hesitate, also, to stop reading if a paper is not worth your efforts. After reading the opening paragraph of a confusingly written essay, I will stop and tell the writer that I'm lost, bored, or confused, and ask the writer to revise only the first portion of the essay and have that portion peer-edited before having another conference with me.
- By becoming your students' editor, you are placing the onus of learning firmly on their shoulders. You are simply a part of their writing process, an important part, mind, but a part that will soon disappear from their lives. By making students peer dependent rather than teacher dependent, you are paving the way for your students to become independent writers.

One-to-Four

Teacher and Classroom Preparation: Make sure that both you and each of the
   students have a copy of the essay.
Length of Time: 30 minutes.

- By introducing collaborative writing (Chapter Four) into your classes,
  you can engage in thorough conferences on a single essay with four
  students at a time. Such conferences become excellent mini-lessons.

Markers

Whenever possible, have someone else do the actual grading of the papers that you have
conferenced. When the results come back, you will still be your students' editor, not
their judge. Together, you can work to improve their writing and when it does improve,
as it surely will, you and the student writer can both rejoice.

If your school does not have a budget to hire markers, try to persuade the
administration to approve one so that you can fully participate in helping your students
improve their writing process. However, if no money is available, consider hiring a
graduate student to mark for you. The money you spend will be worth free weekends,
will save early burnout, will place you firmly on the side of your students, and will help
a struggling graduate student. You can instruct your marker to keep standards high,
and because your marker will not know the students, you can be assured that marks
will be impartial.

Writing Associates or Writing Fellows Programs

Many colleges and some high schools have introduced a student tutoring program in
which able students help less able ones to master writing skills. Writing Associates
(or Writing Fellows) can be high-school students for elementary school writers, twelfth
graders for other high-school students, second- or third-year college students for
freshmen, volunteer parents or senior citizens. In its program on education in
America, *48 Hours* showed how potential high-school dropouts turned around once they
began to tutor elementary students. In addition, the elementary students not only
enjoyed the experience but learned from these almost-lost students.

Once organized, the Writing Associates Program trains a number of high-
achiever English students to help students across the curriculum to improve writing
skills. Sometimes two or three students are assigned to a non-English class and will
edit up to ten students' major writing assignments. Instructors who use Writing
Associates recognize that the quality of their students' papers improves dramatically
in style and mechanics.

Normally, Writing Associates are given either honors awards or cash for their
services.

YOUR OWN PEER-EDITING IDEAS

CHAPTER SIX

Examination Icebreakers

Most students find exams harrowing. Some teachers, too, would abolish examinations if they had their way, sure in the knowledge that sitting for exams interferes with the learning process. But it looks as if exams are here to stay in most school districts. The active-learning teacher tries to make this necessary evil as easy as possible for students, teaching them how to predict what is on the exam, how to prepare for the exam, and exactly what the teachers are looking for in responses to exam questions.

The active-learning teacher will not test pure knowledge and comprehension through true/false, multiple choice, and fill-in-the-blanks questions, which at best rely on sheer memory and at worst often trick students. Rather, students are allowed to bring in their texts, dictionaries, thesauri, notes, journals. Knowing how to use the available material is more important than knowing a few facts that will disappear from short-term memory the day after the exam.

Surely the point of education is to teach and test material that will stay with students, that has some bearing on their lives, that will, in fact, change their lives. Too many students see no significance in the course material, and the exams they have to sit for often prove to them the irrelevancy of the course – a harsh observation, but a true one. I think that all teachers should take a long look at their courses and ask themselves, "Ten years from now, what do I want my students to remember about the material I am teaching?" Your answer to this question might change not only the content of your examination but also your approach to your entire course. Every time I hear students talking about when they "get out" of school, I am reminded that they think of school as a jail, not a pleasant place where they want to be.

When you make up and administer examinations, remember that, in most cases, you are not discovering the true value of your students. Rather, you are proving that some students can write exams; others cannot. Most examinations reveal little about students' learning processes. On the day of the exam, a student might have a headache, be involved in a personal tragedy, be too tired, too nervous, or just have an off day. Or a student may have lucked-out and studied for the exact essay question or unit of material that you assigned. Yes, an examination undervalues our students' progress, but as long as we have to deal with the beast, we can help students to make an unnatural act as pleasant as possible.

Helping Students Prepare for Examinations

Teacher and Classroom Preparation: None required.
Length of Time: 15 minutes

- In groups of three or four, students should make up a set of instructions for their fellow students to follow in preparing for an examination. After they have presented their set of instructions to the whole class, conduct a discussion so that they can hear some ideas they didn't think of – from other groups or from you.

Helping Students Learn Examination Terminology

Teacher Preparation: Duplicate the list of key verbs below, or adapt the list to fit
   your needs
Length of Time: 20 minutes.

• Because the key verb (telling students what to do) is the most important part of
an exam question, you might give them a workshop to determine the exact
meaning of each key verb commonly found in well-constructed exam
questions. Here are some of the key verbs you might give each group. For
each one in the list, I have provided an explanation of its meaning and a
suggestion about what sort of response an examiner would expect.

Exam Key Words

Analyze	means to break down into parts and look at each part critically. (Examine the many key words associated with *analysis*.)
Apply	means to demonstrate your knowledge and understanding of material by using it extensively and confidently in various situations. (Examine the many key words associated with *application*.)
Compare	means to make ideas clear by calling attention to similarities (and sometimes differences) between them. Use specific examples.
Contrast	means to make ideas clear by calling attention to differences between them. Use specific examples.
Define	means to explain the meaning of a particular expression. A definition should be illustrated with at least one specific example.
Describe	means to write about an object or event in some details.
Discuss	is an ambiguous term that you should avoid using.*
Evaluate	means to judge or give your opinion of something. (See the many key words associated with *evaluation*.)
Explain	means to write an expository piece, including clear and concise details.
Illustrate	means to support a point by means of *short*, key quotations and specific references to the work in question.
List	means to jot down points about a subject at random, unless asked to do so in a particular order.
Outline	means to draft a brief plan for a fully developed essay, perhaps with headings and subheadings.
Point out	means to look specifically and precisely at some aspect of a topic.
State	means to be as clear and concise as possible in answering.
Summarize	means to take a larger work or concept and reduce it to its main ideas.
Synthesize	means to blend two or more things you know in order to produce something original. (See the key words associated with *synthesis*.)
Trace	means to arrange items in a meaningful sequence (chronological, climactic, cause/effect).

---

* If you ask students to define *discuss*, they will probably use every term imaginable. The use of
discuss makes students uncertain what kind of response an examiner wants.

Anatomy of an Exam Question

Teacher Preparation: Make up a few exam questions for students to analyze.
Length of Time: 30 minutes.

- Review with the class the art of composing a good exam question. Generally, an exam question should have three parts:
  - a *key word* that tells the students what they are supposed to do,
  - an *object* that tells them what general information to use to perform their task, and
  - a *limiting factor or factors* that tells what specific information to include in the answer
- Here is an example question to help students see the three parts in action:

Sample Exam Question

Point out the methods used by Kate Chopin in "The Story of an Hour," to show how Louise Mallard – while she sits in front of the open window – frees herself of her husband's domination.

Key words: point out
Object: methods to show how Louise Mallard frees herself of her husband's domination
Limiting Factor: refer to a specific part of the story – what happens while she sits in front of the open window

---

- Notice how the question ties the students down fairly specifically. Obviously it would do students no good to refer to a part of the story other than the scene involving Louise in front of the open window. Tell the students that they would be wasting their time if they did so. Before students begin to answer a well-worded question that has three parts, they should read it carefully so that they do no more or less than it tells them to do.
- Instead of using the above question for your students, make up a new one.

YOUR OWN ANALYSIS EXAM QUESTION

- Have students form small groups. Together, they should compose several questions on recent course material, evaluate them, and present one to the class for criticism.
- As a follow-up, students may answer the best question, as an assignment.

Helping Students Predict Examination Questions

Teacher and Classroom Preparation: None required.
Length of Time: 2 or 3 minutes, or as long as you like.

- Encouraging students to keep a daily journal to trace their journey through your course helps them keep the material fresh in their minds. Occasionally, near the beginning of the term, pose a question that tests analysis, application, evaluation, or synthesis skills that will be required on the exam. Suggest that they respond to the question in their journals so that you can edit the answer during the next period. The next day, conduct a Circle Editing or Trio Editing (Chapter 5) session. Later in the term, have the class as a whole predict exam questions. Let them choose one on which to write a journal entry. Finally, near the end of the term, ask pairs of students to predict questions for each other to respond to. Ask the students to bring in the response the next day to have it evaluated by the giver of the question. Students can use the sets of guidelines in Chapter 5 for evaluating answers.

Instant Writing

Teacher Preparation: Have a few exam questions available.
Length of Time: 10 minutes for each session, 5 minutes for evaluation.

- Occasionally, conduct an instant-writing session. For ten minutes students should respond in their journals to a question that you pose. One or two students might volunteer to write on the board or on an overhead transparency so that you can conduct an editing session after ten minutes. For variety, ask a student to pose a question for an instant-writing session, and respond to it yourself on the board or overhead along with the students.
- To encourage students to participate in instant-writing exercises outside of class, hold a session where everyone must come with a question. Have students exchange questions and respond for ten minutes. Afterwards, have them give their responses to the asker for an evaluation.
- After a few mock exams, students should have no trouble using higher-level thinking skills, and exams will be much easier.

Student-Conceived Exams

Teacher Preparation: Compose a "bare bones" exam similar to the one on the next page. Give each student a copy, with the instructions that they are to make up the actual exam question, using one of the key analysis words (Chapter 2). In addition, they should record their name as the examiner. Have them bring the sheet to class the next day.
Length of Time: Depending on the type of exam, anywhere from 10 minutes to an entire period.

Exam

_____
(name)

Read the following poem chosen by _____.

```




```

With specific reference to the text, write a 250-word literary analysis – on separate paper – in response to the following question. (**Make sure your question has a key word, object, and limiting factor.**)

_____

_____

Value: 2 marks   Your mark ___

Your evaluative comments on the essay should justify your mark. Use the Content, Organization, Style, and Usage and Mechanics guidelines* to assist you in evaluating the essay.

Evaluator's comments:

* found in Chapter 5

- On the day of the "exam," collect the completed copies and place them face down on a desk. Invite students to select one – not their own. If necessary, for the first five minutes, students may seek out the "examiner" and ask for clarification of any question. If an examiner makes any changes to the question, he/she must make the change directly on the exam. If students cannot resolve a problem, you might intercede. After five minutes, all students should answer their questions.

- If anyone turns up without a copy of an exam, have a few samples that you have made up available. I usually have a fairly difficult one on hand. Students would far sooner respond to a peer's exam than mine; they won't forget to bring in their copy the next time.

- You have at least two different ways of grading the papers: you can take them home and mark them (this certainly won't be a boring job since every paper will be different.) Or better still, you can have students return their papers to their examiners, who can take home the papers to mark and grade. Since each examiner has to grade only one paper, the papers will receive more time and personal attention than you could give them, and the writers should certainly benefit. (I give students the opportunity to do three of these kinds of exams each term. The first one is out of 2, the second 3, and the third 5. The evaluation training they receive is invaluable; they have a sense of being an important part of the learning community and learn independence. Besides, 2% is hardly going to make or break a student's grade-point average.) If they wish, students can dispute their mark by first taking their paper to their examiner and then to you.

- Application and evaluation exams work just as effectively. By empowering students to make up exams as well as evaluate them, you will change most students' attitudes about exams from one of dread to just another active-learning project.

YOUR OWN IDEAS FOR STUDENT-CONCEIVED EXAMS

- Here is a graded "bare bones" exam. The questions and comments in italics were written entirely by the student examiner, Fred Rink. How would you feel receiving his comments if you were Calvin?

Graded Exam

Name *Calvin Eng*

In an essay of 250 words, answer the following analysis question. Make sure that you support any of your claims with direct reference to *The Unbearable Lightness of Being*.

Point out the social decline of Tomas and Tereza within the background of the changing social atmosphere in which they find themselves.

Question and evaluation by *Fred Rink*

Value: 3 marks   Your mark *2*

Your evaluative comments on the essay should justify your mark. Use the four guidelines to assist you in evaluating the essay.

Evaluator's comments: *Dear Calvin!*

Content: 1 mark out of 1.5
   Nice idea that the country changed the person; however the people changed as a result of their environment. The point of the question was to point out the DECLINE of T and T, which you did attempt, and connect it with the various social backgrounds for each "step" down the ladder. This you also attempted but got lost a bit in the transition from opening paragraph to the main body of your work.
Organization: .3 mark out of .5
   Ideas are there but don't flow too smoothly. Quotations are okay but awkwardly set up.
Style: .3 mark out of .5
   Satisfactory, but your writing (and mine) isn't brilliant. It is just sufficient to get ideas across.
Usage and Mechanics: .3 mark out of .5
   Average, clear but where is the TITLE? (oops I did the same thing!) Learning grammatical variation is difficult, but overall a good effort Therefore 1.9/3

   Thank you for the learning experience.
   If questions, please ask.
   Yours, Fred

- Finally, on many occasions, students rewrite their papers and ask their examiners to re-read their papers. I do not change the marks, but the next time they do another in-class piece of writing, both students and examiners do better. The examiners improve because they "practice what they preach"; the students improve because they have had the opportunity to see and correct their problems.

Second Chance

Teacher Preparation: If you have any students who received less than 50% on
  an examination, prepare a "second chance" exam for them.
Length of Time: Same as the initial exam.

- By allowing students to rewrite another exam worth **half** the value of the
  original, you will give students a second chance by allowing them to bring
  their score up to 50%. In addition, you can help them focus on their problems
  so that they do not repeat the same mistakes. Finally, you can arrange that
  they engage in several dry runs before they rewrite the exam.
- As a dry run, I ask the students to make up four exam questions each,
  following the principles of "Anatomy of an Exam Question." They let me see
  their questions for evaluation. If the questions are all right I gather them and
  then pass out four different questions to each student. If students, while on
  their own, have a free hour, they choose one of the questions, time themselves,
  and write a dry-run exam. Afterwards, they should ask their *sensei* to edit
  the exam for them (See "Karate Kid Walk" in Chapter 5). Completing four
  dry runs *before* they rewrite their exam should ensure that they will write with
  confidence.

YOUR OWN IDEAS FOR WORKSHOPPING EXAMS

Group Teaching and Group Learning

Since introducing active learning into my classes and realizing the importance of setting up a classroom learning community, I enjoy watching the sharing that goes on among the students.

The workshops in this section encourage cooperation among students. Students experience the joys and benefits of cooperative learning. They learn to give and take. They learn to adapt and evaluate. They learn to sift through material, analyzing it for useful information. Finally, they learn to blend material from various sources to produce a synthesis to which they can claim ownership.

As you become familiar with the workshops, you will probably invent variations to fit your students' needs; you might also decide to blend two or more workshops to create a more appropriate one for you.

QUICK REFERENCE TO MOST SUCCESSFUL WORKSHOPS IN SECTION TWO

WORKSHOPS	PAGE

CHAPTER SEVEN

Students as Teachers

The best way to learn something is to teach it to someone else. Asking students to teach other students can be rewarding for both student teachers and learners. Student teachers often bring a freshness and new approach to the all-too-familiar material.

Group Teaching

Teacher Preparation: After students have completed the workshop "Connecting the Thinking Process with Course Content" (Chapter 2), they should be able to present a worthwhile "lesson" as student teachers. So that the first teaching workshop remains painless, divide the class into groups of six or seven. Choose several topics that you wish students to teach.

Length of Time: The lesson will be 15 minutes for each group, but you should give them class time to prepare and research. Often, groups will also use time outside of class to prepare.

- Each group chooses a different topic. The group's task is not only to teach the characteristics and historical background of the topic, but also to introduce several examples. As well, they should encourage students to compose their own examples, following the same style and form as the models.
- For example, during a recent literature class dealing with types of poetry, a group of six students presented an excellent lesson on the cinquain. (Other groups chose to teach such forms as haiku, limericks, acrostics, concrete poems, and quatrains. Poetic forms such as sonnets, lyrics and narratives are too difficult for a first attempt at "teaching.") At the end of their "lesson," each "teacher" took five other students aside, placed them in a row of five desks, and handed each student a piece of paper with a title. Each student in the row was to write a first line, containing two syllables, that would fit the title. The student was to pass the partial cinquain to the next student who was to write a second line (containing four syllables) and pass it on. Then the students wrote the third (six syllables), fourth (eight syllables), and fifth (two syllables) lines. Each group composed five cinquains; the whole class composed thirty. At the end of the 15-minute lesson, all of the students fully appreciated the cinquain.
- By the end of the six subsequent 15-minute lessons, everyone in the room will know and appreciate the types of poems. If, in the future, they forget any of the details, they will be able to call upon one of the six student teachers for help, instead of you.

Hint: Insist that "teachers" not lecture or read notes. Instead, they should fill their lessons with activities in which their "students" can take part. As well, I encourage students not to take notes. Rather, I suggest that they should take ten minutes at home and summarize in their journals what they have learned that day. You might explain to the "student teachers" a bit of the philosophy behind active learning, duplicating the material in the following box or adapting it to fit your needs.

Dialogue

Teacher: How did you get to know your topic? **Student Teacher**: By brain-storming with the other members of our group.

Teacher: Would you say that you know just as much about the topic as I do? **Student Teacher**: I think so.

Teacher: While you were learning about your topic, how did I teach you? **Student Teacher**: You didn't. We learned it by becoming involved.

Teacher: So...? **Student Teacher**: We shouldn't teach our "students." Instead we should involve them so that they learn it on their own more than just listening to us.

Teacher: Therefore, how much will your "students" know about the topic at the end of the workshop. **Student Teacher**: Just about as much as we *and you* know.

- To help you adapt this workshop to fit your grade and subject, list several small units of content that you think groups of six or seven students would be able to teach. You might consider using this workshop to teach facts about rocks, chemical elements, aerobic exercises, nineteenth-century artists, types of sentences (simple, compound, complex, compound/complex), ways to study, or ways to prepare for an exam.

IDEAS FOR GROUP TEACHING

Desktop Teaching

Teacher Preparation: Because terms often get in the way of learning, make a list of those terms that the students should understand perfectly in order to appreciate a particular unit of course content. Duplicate the list of terms, along with instructions for Desktop Teaching similar to those provided on the next page. Adapt it to fit your needs.

Classroom Preparation: Ensure that the desks are against the wall so that students can move freely across the room.

Length of Time: about half an hour.

- Either assign or let students select a term that they wish to master and teach. I suggest they choose a term that they are totally unfamiliar with, so that they will learn as well from the workshop. Encourage students to use any method they wish to "teach" their terms, but tell them the more they can involve their students, the better. My student teachers normally bring props, provide handouts, roleplay, etc. The "teachers" must be prepared to deal with one or more students at a time. Also, they must answer any questions about the term that their students pose.

• On the due date, give students a copy of all of the terms; for example, prior to "getting into" our first novel, my students taught the important terms connected with novel analysis:

Desktop Teaching Novel Terms

Before you do the workshop, draw a line through the terms you already know. **During** the workshop, go to specific student teachers to learn about the terms you don't know. **After** each teaching session, draw a line through the terms you have learned **only** if you feel that you have mastered them. **After** the workshop, circle any terms you still are not familiar with and write, next to them, the student teachers' names so that you can get together with them at another time.

Term	Student Teacher
allusion	
anagnorisis	
archetypal character	
archetypal conflict (& specific conflict)	
archetypal experience	
atmosphere	
climax/anticlimax	
connotation/denotation	
crisis	
dénouement	
empathy/sympathy	
exposition	
flashback/flash forward	
foreshadowing	
hamartia	
hero/antihero	
hubris	
irony & dramatic irony	
motif	
narrator (all kinds) & trusting a narrator	
paradox	
plot/subplot	
point of view (omniscient/limited, first/third person, author's/character's)	
protagonist/antagonist	
satire	
setting (time/place)	
suspense	
symbolism	
structure of novel (different kinds)	
text/subtext	
theme	
tone (direct/ironic)	
tone (objective/subjective)	
verisimilitude	

- On the day of presentation, number off the students 1 to 4. Announce that students 1 and 3 will teach students 2 and 4. After ten minutes, numbers 2 and 4 teach 1 and 3. Then, 1 and 2 teach 3 and 4, and so on. During the final five minutes, allow students to seek out the teachers they need.
- If there are not enough terms for each student, assign the same term to two. It's beneficial for the students to visit two "teachers" dealing with the same difficult term.

Circle Teaching

Teacher Preparation: If you have some facts or terminology that you want your students to know and understand, try this workshop. Make a list of the facts and terms. Divide class into groups of 6 to 8. Assign a different, specific topic to each member of the group. Assign the *same* topics to the members of all the other groups so that each group is working on the same set of topics.

Classroom Preparation: You will need clear areas so that each 6-to-8-student group can stand in a circle.

Length of Time: 10 to 15 minutes.

- Each student should prepare the same number of 3x5 cards as there are members in the group, writing an important but different fact, detail, example, illustration, or comparison about the topic on each separate card. Read together, the cards should contain a complete lesson of the necessary knowledge and comprehension of the topic. Students may have to do some research before they make up the cards.
- On the day of presentation, one student, acting as the "teacher," gives each student in the group one of the cards he/she has prepared. The "teacher" reads the information on the first card dramatically out loud, stressing key words, and adds gestures to reinforce the meaning. All students in the group repeat the material they've just heard from memory, with the "teacher" helping. They should endeavor to stress the same words and gestures as the "teacher" and repeat the information in as dramatic a fashion as the "teacher." Then the student to the right repeats from memory what is on the first card, saying it along with the "teacher"; then reads what is on his/her card (the second card of the series), stressing any word that the "teacher" has underlined and adding an appropriate gesture. All students repeat from memory the contents of the first and second cards with as much emphasis as possible. The third student repeats from memory what is on the first card with the "teacher" and what is on the second card with the previous student, then reads what is on the third card with appropriate emphasis and gesture. The procedure continues in the same way until all the cards have been introduced. At the end, students will be able to recite *with* gestures the entire contents of all cards.
- All groups in the room will be dealing with the same material but with a different "teacher" leading them. The student teachers should be encouraged to have students repeat information if it's not clear enough. And, because students repeat information in order to reinforce it, you should intervene if you hear mispronunciations or errors.

- Here, for example, is what one student teacher presented on seven cards to teach the gerund:

  Card 1: A Gerund is a *verbal*.

  Card 2: A Gerund is like a *verb* and a *noun*.

  Card 3: A Gerund always ends in *i-n-g*.

  Card 4: *Running* is a gerund.

  Card 5: *Laughing* is a gerund.

  Card 6: Two examples of gerunds are: *Seeing* is *believing*.

  Card 7: Three examples of gerunds are: The students gave up *smoking*, *drinking*, and *swearing*.

Hint: you might like to give students a copy of the above example or make up one yourself, to show them how to make up simple examples and details in order for them to complete their 3x5 cards. Don't forget that students are to memorize the content from *all* of the cards, so the simpler the explanations are, the better.

- Once all groups have finished learning the information and feel confident that they "know" it, they should repeat one go-around – with full emphasis and gestures – for the other groups in the room. None will be identical, even though they are all dealing with the same topic. Usually each group receives a round of applause from the other groups because they understand and appreciate the content of the presentation. By listening to what other "teachers" have had their groups learn, the rest of the students can also judge the quality of the learned material. Through class discussion, you can ensure that everyone has learned the correct information.
- Then the procedure continues with the second "teacher's" presentation. For example, if the lesson were on verbals, Teacher Number Two might have Gerundial Phrases; Three might have Participles; Four, Participial Phrases; Five, Infinitives, Six, Infinitive Phrases; and Seven, the differences between Gerunds and Participles.
- As a follow-up, encourage students to write in their journals. Because of the abundance of repetition, students should find no difficulty in recalling the material when they write in their journals and will come away from Circle Teaching with a real feeling of having learned something.
- Circle Teaching workshops work especially well in classes of English as a Second Language. Student teachers, under your guidance, can quickly and thoroughly learn pronunciation, vocabulary, sentence construction, idiomatic expressions, tenses, and all of the other details that foreign students need to know.
- If you have a multicultural classroom, you might like to give opportunities to bilingual students to teach some facts about their language and culture. By taking part in one of the Circle Teaching workshops yourself, you can learn a great deal. For example, while learning to count to ten in Japanese and Chinese, I soon began to appreciate how difficult it is for many of my ESL students to learn an entire new language. Having ESL students teach small units of material related to their culture also helps foster better understanding and appreciation of differences.

Answers or Solutions

Teacher Preparation: On completion of a unit of course content, make up four questions or problems or four partial writing projects – one per paper for a group of 4 students. Duplicate the sheets so that each group will be working on the same questions, problems, or projects. (See samples on the next page.)

Classroom Preparation: Arrange desks in circles of 4.

Length of Time: 20 minutes.

- This workshop allows students to test their knowledge and understanding of course content through application and evaluation strategies.
- Present each student in a group with a different first part of a project: a complex problem, a thesis statement, the result of an experiment, the first step of a how-to manual, a complex mathematical equation, etc. Give the same set of handouts to all the other groups.
- For two or three minutes, each student should work on the first step of the workshop he or she has received. You might give them the following instructions:

> Each time a paper comes to you, you will be asked to provide a solution or an answer. You might have to supply a piece of prose, a stanza of poetry, a drawing, or one or more numbers. As soon as you have done your portion of the answer, pass it to the right. Because you will all have a different project on every paper that comes to you, begin by examining what other students have done. If you find what you think is an error in another student's work, don't hesitate to correct it before you carry on with your part. When you present your answer or solution, you must not repeat those that other students have used. When you hear a signal, the next person who receives the paper must wrap up the workshop with a memorable conclusion.

- When the workshop is over, all members of the group should evaluate all the responses. When they have reached a consensus, they should prepare to share their responses with the other groups who, of course, have been working on the same four problems, experiments, or assignments.
- Answer or Solution workshops allow all students to pick up on each other's learning and thinking processes. Weaker students learn how to improve their thinking and writing strategies.
- Once students do a few of these workshops, have one group make up a set of four problems, thesis statements, etc., for another group. Upon completion, groups should exchange material for a thorough evaluation. Give groups a chance to discuss problems. You may have to mediate disputes and settle arguments, but you will soon discover that this workshop places the responsibility for the learning process firmly on the shoulders of the learners.

- Here are a couple of example handouts for Answer or Solution workshops:

The beginning of an essay

Education Problems

During a speech, President George Bush said that he would like to be known as the Education President. In order to improve education in the United States, the President should first recognize several problems in American schools and present workable solutions for those problems.

    Solution 1:
    Solution 2:
    Solution 3:
    Conclusion:

- The results of this workshop should lead to a good argumentative essay. Because this opening is just one of four that will be passed around, students will be dealing with many government policies. All you have to do is change key words to mention other topics: drugs, gun control, flag burning, disarmament, etc.

Creative Writing: Ballads

Write an opening quatrain with a specific ballad rhythm and rhyme scheme on the character of Macbeth (or any other protagonist or antagonist of a major work that you have studied). After one student has written the opening stanza, the next to the right must compose a second stanza and pass the poem to the right. The last person in the circle composes a concluding stanza.

- The successful results of this will be four different ballads per group. One might deal with Macbeth, another, Lady Macbeth, and others Banquo, Macduff, etc. You can have a follow-up session by having the group evaluate all of the ballads, choose the best one, and present it for the other groups. The group may present it in as dramatic a way as they wish, instead of having just one person reading it to the class. I've had groups act out the entire ballad and thus bring its characters to life.

Enhancement

    Teacher Preparation: At the end of a unit of course content, instruct students, working in pairs, to compose three or four related, simple sentences based on a body of "learned" material. See examples below.
    Length of Time: 10 to 15 minutes.

- Students should exchange their simple sentences with another pair of students. Keeping the simple sentences intact, each pair of students should add enhancements not only to bring the sentences to life but also to compose a single, well-unified paragraph. For example, for a literature class, a pair of students came up with four significant events in the life of Allie Fox (the protagonist from Paul Theroux's *The Mosquito Coast*): Allie Fox went to

Honduras. He compared himself to God. He built Fat Boy. He killed the three strangers.

- Another pair of students came up with the following enhancement:

     Allie Fox, along with his family, *went* by boat *to Honduras* in Central America. Misguided from the start, *he* not only *compared himself to God* but insisted that he was doing a better job in his creation of Jeronimo. Using his own scientific ingenuity, his family, and the natives, *he built* his magnificent ice machine, *Fat Boy*. Allie's downfall began when *he killed the three strangers* by sealing them in Fat Boy and blowing it and them up.

- Another pair came up with the following simple sentences in a history class: Hitler rose to power. He overran Europe. He lost the war. He died.
- Enhancement helps students dig more deeply into the learned material to provide verbal enrichment for basic statements.

TV Game Show

Teacher Preparation: Because most students are familiar with TV game shows, divide the class into groups of four with the suggestion that each group set a body of learned material in the form of one of the popular shows (*Jeopardy!*, *Win, Lose, or Draw*, *Wheel of Fortune*, etc.). Each group should attempt to prepare a different TV game show.

Student Preparation: At home, each member of the group should compose as many questions as possible. When the members of the group meet, they share questions so that each member adds to his/her list. Ultimately, each member has the same list of questions and is ready to "MC" the game.

Classroom Preparation: Create four areas in the room so that you have four shows going on at one time. That way, all students participate.

Length of Time: Depends on how many questions the students make up, but ask students to make up enough questions for a 15-minute show.

- Each member of each group MCs the game with one quarter of the class. By having each game simultaneously played by four groups, all students will get many opportunities to play. Remember, each MC will be asking the same questions.
- By starting each class with a different 15-minute TV game show, within a week everyone in the class will have had a chance to be both an MC and a contestant five or six times.

OTHER IDEAS FOR STUDENTS AS TEACHERS

CHAPTER EIGHT

Brainstorming with Graphics

Working with grids, charts, clusters, and other graphics helps students to organize their thoughts. In many cases students can use a well-organized graphic to write a major paper, solve a complex problem, and ensure that their thinking is thorough and coherent.

Senses Grid

Teacher Preparation: Make up a sample grid similar to the one below. Be sure you include images that evoke the five senses.
Length of Time:10 minutes.

- Start grid work on a simple level so that students can see the usefulness of the activity. For example, when I deal with the importance of images in poetry, I will divide the class into groups of five or six and provide the following grid:

1 rooster crows	laughter of children	groans of agony
2 sun peeps over barn	a mile of sandy beach	room full of weight machines
3 heavy fragrance of hay	marshmallows burning over open fire	beads of sweat
4 bitter flavor of morning coffee	drinking the last dregs of hot cocoa	salty top lips
5 nippy frost the air	balmy trade winds blow the palms	warm flesh on cold metal

- To help students read the grid, ask, "What do the first three entries across have in common?" After some discussion, students will see that they are all sounds. Repeat the same question for the other four entries. Students will soon see that the grid illustrates all five senses: sound, sight, smell, taste, and touch.

- Then ask students to read down the three columns to see if they can determine a setting for the five sense entries. They should try to determine in their setting place, time, mood, atmosphere, and characters.
- As a follow-up, they might attempt to include all the images in a few lines of poetry that they share within their group. Each group might also want to share one poem with the rest of the class.
- For the next class, students should bring in a similar grid that they have composed by themselves, using examples from all five senses. When they come in, have each student number his or her grid. Place the Senses Grids around the room, and have students move from grid to grid to determine the three settings of each Senses Grid. On completion, have the originator of each grid provide the three settings to see if the rest of the students discovered them. Discussion can follow as to why some of the settings were harder to determine than others. Think about applying the Senses Grid across the curriculum; for example, main features of three geographical locations, three entrées, three historical events, etc.
- Students can end the Senses Grid workshop by composing a poem using one of the columns and sharing it with the whole class.

Partial Grid

Teacher Preparation: Make up a partial grid that you wish students to complete.
Length of Time: 5 to 10 minutes.

- This workshop works along the same lines as the Senses Grid above, except that each group works to complete the grid. For example, ask students to complete this Partial Math Grid.

1	4		10
6	9		
11			
16			

- Make up Partial Grids for geography, history, home economics, physical education, or ESL classes. For example: for an ESL class, a Partial Verb Tense Grid would be helpful. You could have Past, Present, and Future tenses illustrated. As a follow-up, students would have to compose sentences in all three tenses. Then, all students would have to bring in their own Partial Verb Tense Grid for their classmates to work out during the next class. In order that students not repeat the same verbs, you might number off students and say, "Numbers 1 to 4 must make up irregular verbs beginning with letters *a* to *e*. Numbers 5 to 8, *f* to *k*." And so on.

Partial Brainstorming Graphics

Teacher Preparation: Develop your own partial Brainstorming Graphic or use one of the examples below.
Length of Time: 10 minutes per graphic.

- Students often find brainstorming with others easier than coming up with ideas and support on their own. Brainstorming with grids, charts or clusters encourages students to think in an organized way. They can use these graphics for comparing and contrasting one thing or person with another, searching for causes of a particular effect, researching an essay, building up enough support for a thesis, gathering reasons, etc.
- Arrange students in groups of three. Give them a copy of a partial graphic and ask them to complete it by adding to the existing brainstorming notes.

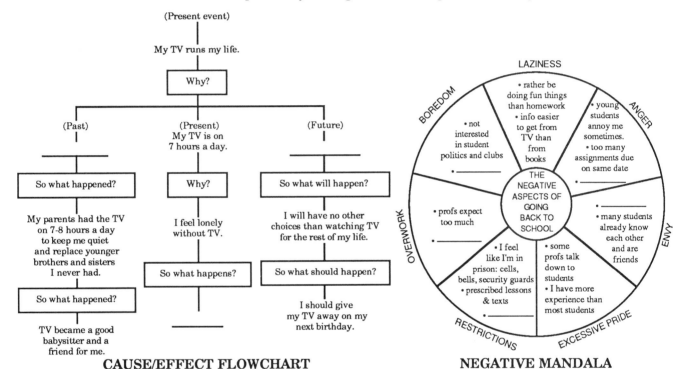

CAUSE/EFFECT FLOWCHART   NEGATIVE MANDALA

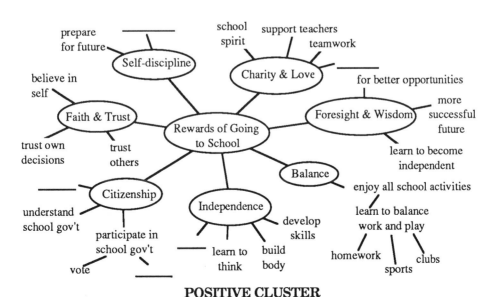

POSITIVE CLUSTER

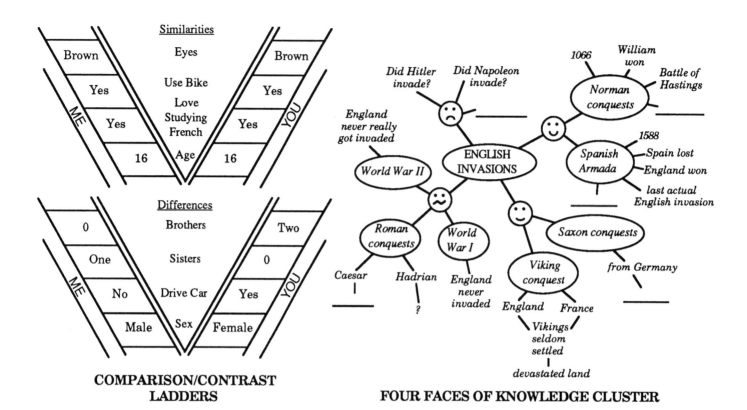

COMPARISON/CONTRAST LADDERS

FOUR FACES OF KNOWLEDGE CLUSTER

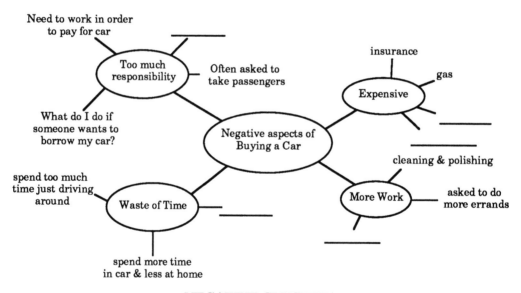

NEGATIVE CLUSTER

• As a follow-up, ask groups to compose a partial Brainstorming Graphic and give it to the group to their right. That group must brainstorm in order to complete the Graphic, and return it to the group on their left. Discussion should follow.

Brainstorming with Graphics

Teacher Preparation: Make up blank graphics based on a portion of your course content or duplicate the ones below.
Length of Time: 20 to 30 minutes per graphic.

- Encourage groups of students to complete a graphic so that they can see the benefits of brainstorming. They will begin to realize that "None of us is as smart as all of us."

Comparison/Contrast Ladders

For this graphic, choose as your topic something that you wish to learn, such as how to read a novel, play a guitar, do a math problem, prepare for an exam, etc. Assume that you have been asked to write an essay on the best and the worst ways to perform this activity. Fill in the two ladders with as much supporting evidence as you can think of. Decide on which rung of the ladder to place the evidence, and, if you place something on one ladder, think of something to place on the opposite rung of the other ladder.

The thing you wish to learn: _____

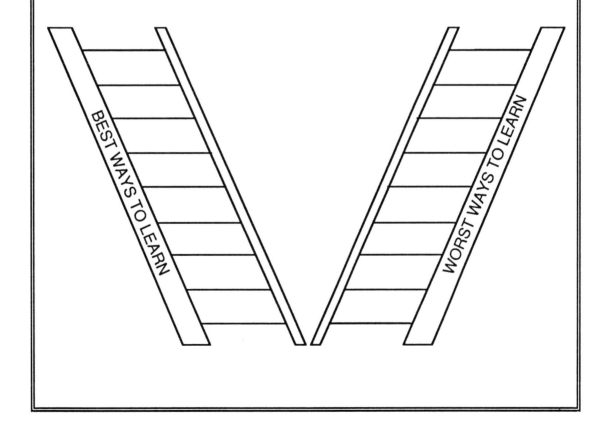

Mandala

On the outside of each section of the mandala, print four inventions that have significantly changed the world (the wheel, photography, the atomic bomb, computer chip, and so on). Within each wedge, include two or three ways in which the invention changed the world.

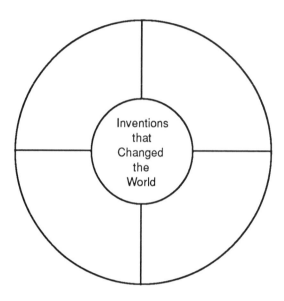

As a follow-up, fill in the following blanks.

a. If you used the mandala to organize facts for an essay, what method of organization would you use in the essay: cause/effect, reason/result, climactic, chronological, or another method? _____

b. What type of supporting evidence would you use for each invention (details, facts, examples, quotations, or other)?

invention 1 _____   invention 2 _____
invention 3 _____   invention 4 _____

c. Complete the following outline, assuming that you will write the essay based on your mandala:

SIGNIFICANT INVENTIONS

I.   Introduction   IV.
II.   A.
      A.   B.
      B.   V.
III.   A.
      A.   B.
      B.   C.
                             VI. Conclusion

• As a follow-up, assign a complex project that requires intensive brainstorming. Encourage students to construct graphics in order to develop plenty of support for their project. You might ask students to submit their graphics along with their completed projects.

YOUR OWN IDEAS FOR BRAINSTORMING WITH GRAPHICS

Character Traits

Teacher Preparation: Duplicate the graphic below or adapt one to fit your needs. After a unit of course content, choose one or more people (actual or fictional) from a body of material for your students to analyze.
Length of Time: 10 minutes for each graphic.

Each of the two opposing character traits on the graphic is separated by a broken line. If the person you are analyzing possesses either the trait or its opposite to some degree, place an **x** along the broken line at about the place which shows how much of the trait the person possesses. For example, if you think the person is *very* clever, place an **x** close to the word *clever* on the broken line.

stupid   –––––––––––––––––––**x**––––   clever

Character Traits of _____

stupid	––––––––––––––––––––––––	clever
impractical	––––––––––––––––––––––––	practical
dull	––––––––––––––––––––––––	interesting
introverted	––––––––––––––––––––––––	extroverted
ugly	––––––––––––––––––––––––	good-looking
aggressive	––––––––––––––––––––––––	cautious
secretive	––––––––––––––––––––––––	open
tells lies	––––––––––––––––––––––––	truthful
chaotic	––––––––––––––––––––––––	organized
untrustworthy	––––––––––––––––––––––––	trustworthy
unathletic	––––––––––––––––––––––––	athletic
fun-loving	––––––––––––––––––––––––	serious
unmechanical	––––––––––––––––––––––––	mechanical
	––––––––––––––––––––––––	
	––––––––––––––––––––––––	
	––––––––––––––––––––––––	
	––––––––––––––––––––––––	

- Invite students to add to the grid opposing characteristics that apply to the person they are analyzing.
- As a follow-up, ask students to discover the main character trait of the subject. If they cannot, they should repeat the workshop, concentrating on adding further opposing characteristics to the graphic.
- This workshop will work for places and things as well as people. Ask students to make up a suitable graphic for places and things. Afterwards, choose subjects from a body of material that they have studied so that they can discover important characteristics of the place or thing. Possible subjects could be South Africa, Miami, Hollywood, computers, the War of 1812, the metric system, igneous rocks, etc.

YOUR OWN IDEAS FOR GRAPHIC WORKSHOPS

CHAPTER NINE

Debates

By debating the relationship of course content to their own lives, students quickly show you what they are getting out of the course. Debaters need a thorough knowledge and understanding of the material before they can demonstrate their ability to evaluate it. Debating significant sections of course material will not only develop students' higher-level thinking skills but also make the course more relevant to their lives.

If your students are unfamiliar with debating practices, you might first introduce them to the Personal Pro/Con workshop.

Personal Pro/Con

Teacher Preparation: After you have demonstrated the Personal Pro/Con
    workshop with a student volunteer, divide students into pairs.
Length of Time: 3 or 4 minutes for each Personal Pro/Con workshop.

- One student gives the other a general topic to encourage personal opinions: babies, women, men, school, religion, war, TV, etc. As soon as the student hears the topic, he/she must speak *for* the topic to the other student, presenting all the positive arguments. After a short time, perhaps 30-45 seconds, the listener should clap, and immediately the speaker should speak *against* the topic, presenting all the negative arguments. After a short time, the listener should clap and the speaker should immediately present more "pro" arguments. (Encourage students to change sides in mid-sentence without using "but.") Another clap and the speaker presents more "con" arguments. This process should continue for two or three minutes with the speaker changing quickly from speaking *for* to speaking *against* the topic.
- Reverse positions and have the new listener present a new topic.
- Then repeat the workshop one more time, giving each student a chance to talk for or against a personal topic.
- With all students engaged in the Personal Pro/Con workshop at the same time, the noise level can be quite intense, but this will not bother the students because they are concentrating on what they are saying to each other. If possible, you might send students to different areas around the campus, even outside – with the instructions to be back in the class in 15 minutes. During that time, each should engage in at least two Pro/Con workshops.
- When each pair has gone through the workshop twice and the class has reassembled, you might have a few volunteers share their Personal Pro/Con workshop with the whole class. Because of the speed of delivery, the repeat workshop will not be the same as the original, but it will be fun for the class to see a few pairs in action.

Formal Pro/Con

Teacher Preparation: Administer this workshop in the same way as the Personal Pro/Con workshop, except that the topics must be course oriented. Therefore, devise a few suggested topics linked to your course content to help the students think of their own.

Length of Time: 3 or 4 minutes for each Formal Pro/Con workshop.

- After studying a few pieces of literature, my English students will give names of characters, poets, films, novels, or authors as topics. The task of the speaker is to think of all the "pro" characteristics of the subject until the clap; then all of the "con" characteristics until the next clap; and so on. Because Pro/Con workshops work best at high intensity, they also develop higher-level thinking skills at high speed. You might suggest that while speaking, students should not repeat themselves; this rule encourages concentration and deeper insight into the topic. Dealing with a historical figure's good and bad points, for example, can produce an excellent character sketch – and the exercise can serve as an effective brainstorming technique for a comparison/contrast piece of writing. Again, when each pair of students has gone through the workshop twice, you might have a few volunteers share their Formal Pro/Con workshop with the whole class. The workshop can serve as an interesting and useful review of a body of course content.
- Needless to say, you can apply the Formal Pro/Con workshop to any course in order to get students to think on their feet. Therefore, consider the Formal Pro/Con workshop for a debate on historical personalities, events, geographical locations, world leaders, laws, theories, etc.

IDEAS FOR ADDITIONAL FORMAL PRO/CON WORKSHOPS

Mini-Personal Debate

Teacher Preparation: Make up a list of 20 or so statements that require a True or False response. (See sample below.)

Length of Time: 20 to 30 minutes.

- Working alone, each student should place "True" or "False" beside each statement. Tell them they cannot use "sometimes," "maybe," or "at times."

- Then, students should go about the room to link up with one student who is definitely on the other side of an argument they feel strongly about. For a few minutes let students try to convince each other that they are right and that their opponent is wrong.
- The list of statements can be as outrageous as you and your students feel comfortable with. For example:
    - Men should be entitled to parental leave.
    - Women are emotionally weaker than men.
    - Men are definitely weaker than women.
    - There is nothing wrong with interracial marriages.
    - There's nothing wrong with bisexuality.
    - Euthanasia for the terminally ill is all right.
- As a follow-up, find out how many students were able to convince an opponent to change his/her mind.

Mini-Formal Debate

Teacher Preparation: Administer the Mini-Formal Debate in the same way as the Personal one, but make up statements based on the course content. (See sample below.)

Length of Time: 20 to 30 minutes.

- For my literature class, for example, I composed the following list:
    - *The Handmaid's Tale* is Margaret Atwood's best novel to date.
    - Offred does not escape at the end of the novel.
    - The Commander is impotent.
    - Orwell's *1984* is a better novel than *The Handmaid's Tale*.
    - The novel of *The Handmaid's Tale* is much better than the film version.
- Making up similar statements for your course material will help students think and talk about what they have learned. The Mini- Formal Debate can also serve as a worthwhile review lesson.
- Consider using the Mini-Formal Debate with such topics as
    - Napoleon was a better general than Wellington
    - Using the metric system is easier than using the imperial system
    - The Dewey Decimal System is more comprehensive than the Library of Congress System

IDEAS FOR ADDITIONAL MINI-FORMAL DEBATES

Full Debate

Teacher Preparation: Spend a bit of time talking about formal debate procedures. You might like to duplicate the rules of debate below and give them to your students, or, if you wish, modify them to fit your needs. Afterwards, with your class, discuss and select a suitable debate topic (either personal, social, political, or one related to course content). Finally, set a date for the debate, choose students for each side, choose a chairperson and let him/her decide the best way to set up the room for the actual debate.

Length of Time: Two or three days for preparation. One period for the debate.

Rules of Debate

You are about to participate in a formal debate – one in which you and one other student can argue your point of view for or against an issue while two other students who disagree with you will argue that their point of view is correct.

Before the Debate

1. With another student, choose one of the following debate topics (or make up one of your own) with which you strongly agree or disagree. Your topic should be worded as a formal resolution.

   Resolved: that team sports in school should be abolished
   Resolved: that AIDS patients should be quarantined
   Resolved: that final examinations should be abolished
   Resolved: that capital punishment should be reinstated
   Resolved: that violent movies should be censored

   If you make up your own debate topic, make sure that
   a) you can state it as a formal proposition (a statement rather than a question) that begins with "Resolved: that..."
   b) it is a topic that you can debate. One side must be able to say "Yes"; the other, "No." Therefore, there must be good material available for both sides to debate. The more controversial the topic, the better the debate.
   c) it is an interesting issue for both sides as well as those who listen to and judge the debate.
   d) it is a topic that is within your experience, ability, or interest.

2. In formal, interschool debating championships, teams can be assigned to argue on the affirmative side even if they support the negative side, and vice versa. To really test your debating skills, you may want to deal with a proposition that you do not agree with. You will be judged on how well you present your argument, how convincing you are, and a number of other points that are illustrated in the "After the Debate" section.

3. Begin to brainstorm and research facts and arguments to support your position. To build a strong case, both partners should research, then exchange and share information.

⇨

4. Once you have researched the specific issues in your debate topic, organize the facts so that they will support and prove your position. Outline your arguments and supporting evidence, and divide your arguments between the two speakers.

5. Practice with each other by debating the issue, with one person taking the affirmative side; the other, the negative. The one who is taking the negative position should be particularly forceful. Debates are often won or lost on the debaters' ability to refute what their opponents say. During this practice session, the negative side should try to discover whether the affirmative side is guilty of any imprecise thinking and insufficient proof. After your mock debate, go over your notes again to make sure that you plug all the holes of your argument. Help each other.

6. The next time you and your partner are engaged in a debate, you will be on the **same** side. Remember, in a debate, you are out to convince the judges and listeners, as well as your opponents, of the soundness of your arguments.

The Debate

Use the following suggestions to conduct your debate:

1. You might want to appoint
   a) a chairperson who will maintain order, introduce the resolution, present the speakers in the correct order, and act as timekeeper.
   b) judges to score the debate. Each should score individually. (See "After the Debate" for details and a sample scorecard.)

2. During the debate, each speaker should make a constructive argument and support his/her position. As well, each speaker should make a rebuttal, arguing against what the previous speaker has said. Debates may be conducted in the following order:
First affirmative speaker	four-minute constructive speech
First negative speaker	one-minute rebuttal + four minutes
Second affirmative speaker	one-minute rebuttal + four minutes
Second negative speaker	one-minute rebuttal + four minutes
First affirmative speaker	one-minute (only) rebuttal and summary

3. The following details will help all four speakers follow the content and sequence of a formal debate.

First Affirmative
   Introduce the resolution clearly. State the affirmative's position. For example, "We, the affirmative, agree with the resolution that..."
   Outline the arguments that the affirmative debaters will present. For example, "We will prove this to you by examining A, B, C, D, and E."
   Prove the first one or two arguments by using examples, statistics, testimony, etc. For example, "I will begin by proving that..."
   Summarize your stand and restate the resolution.

⇨

First Negative
> Introduce your position by restating the resolution from your point of view. For example, "We, the opposition, disagree totally with the resolution that.... We believe that..."
> In your rebuttal, attempt to indicate any faulty arguments of the first affirmative speaker. (You will need to take notes during your opponent's speeches so that you have exact details.)
> Restate the resolution from your point of view.
> Outline the arguments that the negative side will present.
> Prove the first few arguments by using examples, statistics, testimony, etc.
> Summarize your stand and restate the resolution.

Second Affirmative
> Restate the resolution.
> In your rebuttal, disprove the arguments of the first negative speaker.
> Restate the resolution.
> Summarize the arguments already made by your colleague.
> Prove your last and strongest arguments.
> Summarize your stand and restate the resolution.

Second Negative
> Restate the resolution.
> In your rebuttal, disprove the arguments of the second affirmative speaker.
> Restate the resolution.
> Summarize your stand by listing the arguments used by your colleague.
> Prove your last and strongest arguments.
> Summarize your stand by listing the arguments used by your side and restate the resolution.

First Affirmative
> Restate the resolution.
> In your rebuttal, disprove the arguments of the second negative speaker.
> Restate the resolution.
> Summarize your stand by listing the arguments used by your side.
> Restate the resolution.

After the Debate

Here are some suggestions for evaluating a debate:

1. Appoint judges to evaluate the debaters. Divide a piece of paper into four columns. Head the first column "Content," the second "Organization," the third "Presentation," and the fourth, "Total." Then divide the paper horizontally into four parts to correspond to the two Affirmative debaters and the two Negative debaters. Label these parts "1A," "1N," "2A," and "2N." Your scorecard will look something like this:

⇨

	Content	Organization	Presentation	Total
1A				
1 N				
2A				
2 N				

2. As you listen carefully to each speaker (perhaps making notes on a separate sheet of paper if you wish), pay attention both to what a speaker says and to how he/she says it. Give each speaker a score in each category ranging from 0 for very poor to 5 for excellent. Use the following questions to help you judge each category:

Content: Did each point the speaker made relate clearly and directly to the resolution? Did the speaker clearly understand the resolution? Were all arguments well supported with specific evidence? If speakers were arguing in rebuttal, did they answer all the opponent's important points? Did speakers avoid undesirable tactics such as name-calling or insults?

Organization: Were arguments arranged clearly and in a particular order? Were important arguments stressed? Did any speakers leave loose ends or unsettled arguments? Did speakers obey the rules established for the debate concerning time of speeches, order of speaking, etc.? Were speakers on time and prepared?

Presentation: Did speakers *present* their arguments to the audience, judges, and opponents rather than *reading* from notes? Could they be heard and understood clearly? Did they speak with enthusiasm? Were their gestures effective and natural? Were they courteous and interested while others were speaking? Were they courteous to the chairperson, judges, and their opponents?

3. When you have made your judgment of each speaker and calculated your totals, give your evaluation sheet to the chairperson. He/she will add up the scores of all the judges and announce the winner.

4. Alternately, the chairperson may take a vote of the judges and audience *before* and *after* the debate. The number of people who change their minds on the issue *may* determine the winner.

5. Whether you win or lose the debate, you will learn a great deal from your participation; your composing, speaking, and listening skills will be greatly improved.

Formal Debating Across the Curriculum

• Using the procedure outlined in the above Formal Debate, choose propositions relating to history, geography, or any other course across the curriculum.For example,

Resolved: that South Africa would be a stronger country if apartheid were abolished

Resolved: there is life on at least one other planet

Resolved: that calculators not be used in math exams

YOUR OWN DEBATING IDEAS

CHAPTER TEN

Invitations

Teachers have long invited members of the outside community as experts or as assistants to help focus students' attention on real issues. Instead of your inviting guests to the classroom, you might consider having students invite the guests. The following are just a sampling of ways for students to enrich their workshops by interviewing outside guests and, possibly, inviting them to the classroom.

Knowing Your Campus

Teacher Preparation: Make up a worksheet of questions as described below.
Length of Time: One period.

- This workshop is designed to give new students a sense of belonging.
- Form students into groups of three. Give each group a worksheet of questions about the campus and send them out to find the answers. Make sure that each set of questions is different; otherwise, several groups will move around together. The questions might be in the form of a treasure hunt. For example, ask each group to begin at a different campus location and end with their arranging to invite to class at a later date an individual who works in the school: principal, vice-principal, dean, department head, nurse, doctor, counsellor, custodian, cook, president of the PTA, secretary, audio/visual expert, librarian. Make sure that you have notified everyone on your list about your treasure hunt. If any cannot come to your class, ask the group to interview each and report its findings to the class.
- General example questions for the treasure hunt may range from the number of bathrooms in the school to its founding date. Specific questions which will lead students to an individual may range from asking the room number of a particular counsellor to asking (after students have met him/her) the number of students a counsellor serves.

Inviting the Expert

Teacher Preparation: Read over the following material.
Length of Time: Because students will need to seek out experts, they will need to do this outside of class time. Decide how much class time you will allow for the actual presentations.

- Suggest that each group of students invite an expert to class. You could connect this project with a "Career Day" by asking students to invite people from several occupations: scientists, journalists, lawyers, cooks, teachers, mechanics, dental technicians, etc. If it's not possible to bring all these

guests to the classroom, encourage students to videotape an interview with the guest to show the class.
- For students who need help in interviewing techniques, duplicate (or modify) the following set of guidelines:

Interviewing Techniques (part 1)

Before the Interview

- Consider the purpose of the interview: what do you want to know? Also, consider what your audience of fellow students will want to know.
- Spend some time watching professional interviewers. Note how they discover useful information about their subjects and at the same time keep their audiences interested and entertained. Do you have a favorite interviewer?
- If possible, do a bit of reading about your subject beforehand so that you can ask good questions. Your interviewee will appreciate your consideration, and both of you will save time.
- Compose several open-ended questions – that is, ones that require more than a "yes" or "no" answer. For example: "How did you first become interested in...?"
- Consider how you are going to record your interview. You may just talk and make notes afterwards; take a pad and pencil with you and jot notes down as you talk; or use an audio or a video recorder. Remember to check with the interviewee **before** you set up a recorder. Why? Some interviewees may even object to your taking notes. Why?

During the Interview

- Your first job will be to make the interviewee feel at ease. What general questions at the beginning of the interview might help your subject (and you) relax?
- Try to have a conversation with your subject instead of looking at your list of questions. Do, however, bring the questions with you. If there's a lull in the conversation, you can use one of your questions to get the interview back on track.
- Keep the reporter's interviewing techniques in mind. Ask who-where-when-what-why-how questions.
- Once the interview is running smoothly, do not hesitate to ask for clarification: "Please define that term. Would you elaborate? What did you mean by that?" If you become confused, you might repeat a piece of information in your own words so that the interviewee can verify that you have understood.

- Instead of or in addition to the live class interview, you might have the students produce a written, publishable interview. Give them a copy of the following guidelines or adapt them to fit your needs.

Interviewing Techniques (part 2)

After the Interview

- The actual interview might not have flowed in a logical order, but you must organize your written interview. Consider leaving out information that is not helpful or interesting for your audience.
- Generally, a written interview is not a word-for-word report; it's a piece that contains the best parts of the interview in a logical order.
- You might wish to draft an opening in order to set up the interview for your reader, mentioning necessary background, setting (including time, place, and atmosphere), and any other information that you think your audience should know before reading the interview.
- Decide whether you are going to draft your interview as a straightforward question-and-answer piece or a narrative-and-dialogue story. Notice the difference between these two examples, based on an interview with playwright Beverley Simons. Which do you prefer? Why?

Question and Answer

Interviewer: Can you talk a little bit about how you work? Do you have a routine or do you just wake up in the morning and decide that today is a day you might write?

Simons: Well, it depends what stage of work I'm at. Putting the words on paper is usually the last step. It's a process that starts somehow at the back of my head. Sometimes it starts with a character who suddenly appears and I don't know why. It may be a scene. It may be something that's angered me or excited me. Usually, I'll make notes on it and then put them away. A major piece for me extends over four or five years like this.

Interviewer: Does it take you that long to write a play?

Simons: Of course not. I do not consciously...

Narrative and Dialogue

I asked Beverley Simons to tell me a little bit about how she worked. "Do you have a routine or do you just wake up in the morning and decide that today is a day you might write?"

"Well," Simons answered, "it depends what stage of work I'm at." She paused, and then continued forcefully, "Putting the words on paper is usually the last step. It's a process that starts somehow at the back of my head. Sometimes it starts with a character who suddenly appears and I don't know why. It may be a scene. It may be something that's angered me or excited me. Usually, I'll make notes on it and then put them away. A major piece for me extends over four or five years like this."

"Does it take you that long to write a play?" I enquired.

"Of course not. I do not consciously..."

- After you compose your written interview, make sure to have it edited before you present it to your intended audience.

Interviewing Across the Curriculum

Teacher Preparation: After completing a unit of course content, you might like to make up a list of suitable subjects (real or fictitious) for an interview. Ask students to form pairs: **A** students will be the interviewers; **B** students, the interviewees.
Length of Time: About 10 minutes.

- After choosing a subject, students may need to do some research in order to prepare to be interviewed.
- Using the above interviewing suggestions, **A** interviews **B**, who should adopt the persona of the subject. You can have all the students interviewing at the same time, or you can ask for a volunteer pair who will conduct the interview in front of the rest of the class.
- This workshop will encourage students to dig deep into the personalities, work, contributions, and so on of historical, literary and scientific subjects. As a more imaginative interview, you might make up a list of non-human interviewees: a country, a plant, a chemical element, a planet, a mathematical symbol, an animal, etc. **B** must accordingly adopt the persona of a non-human, but one who can talk.

Trials

Teacher Preparation: Read the suggestions below.
Length of Time: As much as you wish.

- One school I visited has built up a tradition that keeps the whole town buzzing: each year the English department puts one of the main characters from a piece of literature on trial. From the community, prosecution and defense lawyers and a judge come to speak to the senior students who are to be involved in the trial. The students are all assigned specific parts and are expected to prepare accordingly. Besides playing lawyers and judge, students become witnesses for the prosecution and defense, jury members, court personnel, and, of course, the character on trial. The English department makes arrangements with the courthouse staff so that they can take over a large courtroom for one evening. The public fill the galleries and the "Trial of Macbeth" begins as witness after witness takes the stand.
- You can easily put both living and dead personalities on trial. Choose from politics (Hitler), science (Copernicus), philosophy (Socrates), history (John Wilkes Booth), physical education (Ben Johnson), or a suitable subject from your course content

Open House

Teacher Preparation: Read the suggestions below.
Length of Time: As much as you wish.

- Open houses have been popular for a long time. You might consider a mini-open house for the parents of your students. Instead of presenting only written projects for parents to see, you might like to present some of the most successful active-learning workshops for the parents to witness. After seeing the students involved in many of the higher-level thinking workshops, parents will surely see the benefits of active learning.

Senior Helpers

Teacher Preparation: Read the suggestions below.
Length of Time: As much as you wish.

- Writing many assignments is the only way students will improve their writing style. The thought of marking all those assignments will daunt the most ambitious of teachers. Indeed, a heavy marking load often destroys many teachers' joy in teaching.
- By setting up editing groups of four or five students, you might discover a way to alleviate the marking pressure. Ask that each group invite one senior citizen from their community to join their editing group to help them with their written assignments. If you provide editing guidelines to the seniors, they can comment on, evaluate, and make revision suggestions on the papers within their editing group. Such a project not only will help your students and you but will often provide an exhilarating diversion for a senior and lessen the generation gap.
- Two or three times during the term, you might ask students to hand you one of their many assignments, the one they think is their best. You can grade this single paper. From the results, you might adjust your guidelines to ensure that your students and their "senior" editors attend more closely to some details.

Graduate Helpers

Teacher Preparation: Read the suggestions in "Senior Helpers" above.
Length of time: As much as you wish.

- You or your students might invite interested graduates with a gift for writing to serve as editors. Following the same instructions as in the "Seniors" section, you will find yet another way to ease your marking load.

Graduate Tutors

Teacher Preparation: Approach a few of your "A" graduates and ask them if they would consider tutoring.

- Consider asking graduates to become tutors for your poorer students. I always have at least four ex-students available to tutor students who are having difficulties with course material. In fact, I insist that some ESL students use the services of a tutor simply to become more familiar with English. Students and tutors meet outside of class time and make their own arrangements about schedules and fees.
- With the help of these graduate tutors, students who might otherwise fail your course will demonstrate remarkable improvement.
- Having graduates as tutors will help your present students greatly because graduates
  - know the course material
  - know your expectations
  - will be able to communicate with your students as both authorities and peers
  - serve as excellent liaisons between you and your students

• Over the years many of my tutors have enjoyed helping students so much that they have decided to become teachers themselves.

IDEAS FOR MORE INVITATIONS

CHAPTER ELEVEN

Jigsaw Workshops

Even though the term "jigsaw" has recently come into use among devotees of active learning, most teachers have already used one or more forms of jigsawing. Thirty years ago, I would occasionally have my sixth graders engage in group work; I would give each group ten minutes at the front of the room to present their findings on a particular topic.

Since discovering the benefits of active learning, I have used so many variations of jigsawing in my classes that I could quite easily devote an entire term to the jigsaw and its variations and **never repeat myself**.

In jigsaw workshops, students assume a large portion of responsibility for their own learning, and share what they have learned with their peers. During a jigsaw workshop you will be free to act as a resource person or a facilitator of students' learning processes, or use the time to meet students in one-to-one tutorial sessions to go over major assignments. Jigsawing will free you from lecturing and always "being in charge." Depending on how deeply you wish to go into a topic, you can have the students demonstrate their powers of analysis, application, evaluation, and synthesis during the presentations of their jigsaw workshops.

Jigsaw workshops allow students to
- become independent learners
- convey existing information
- discover new information
- clarify their thoughts
- refine their ideas
- take ownership of their ideas and insights

The basic Jigsaw has two parts: the Authority Group and the Presentation Group. Before you present either a basic Jigsaw workshop or one of the many variations to your students, read over the characteristics of the Authority and Presentation Groups.

Procedure for the Authority Group

1. You assign a unit of the course content: a novel, several experiments, a country, a political party, a portion of a textbook, a collection of poems, etc. Students must come to the first day of the workshop knowing and understanding (to the best of their ability) the assigned material.

2. Students form Authority Groups of four each. Either you assign the groupings or allow students to get into their own groups. Another way of grouping is to put a grid on a piece of paper on a bulletin board and ask students to sign up under a topic that interests them. The four students who sign under a particular topic automatically become an Authority Group.

TOPICS									
S T U D E N T S	1								
	2								
	3								
	4								

Read vertically for eight Authority Groups working on eight different topics.

3. If you do not wish to assign a topic, you might allow each Authority Group to come up with a different one. The topics should encourage students to develop their higher-level thinking skills: analysis, application, evaluation, and synthesis. Let students know when and how long their presentations will be, so that they can prepare accordingly. Depending on the size of the topic, presentations can last anywhere from five to thirty minutes.

4. If you have 32 students in your class (though I hope you have fewer!), you will have eight Authority Groups, each with a different topic. If you have one or two students more, you can easily put 5 into an Authority Group; with one or two fewer students, you can make an Authority Group of 3.

5. You might give each group a different handout of questions on their own topic, specific instructions that will help them in their presentation, or some other guide to help them become authorities on their topic. (For sample handouts to Authority Groups, see below.) At home, each member of the group should reflect on the topic in a personal way, for example, by writing a journal entry to respond to the topic. Each student should bring this journal entry to the first meeting of the Authority Group and share it with the others in the group. After all members share their reflections, the group can then discuss the topic, shape the main points, organize material, decide whether more supporting data are necessary, determine who should do more research, suggest any visual aids that will make the presentation clearer, etc. Also, encourage the group to invite you to a session to clarify problems; however, do not provide solutions. Rather, help the students to ask the right questions so that they can find their own answers. If you have a lot of relevant material, share it with the group. Or, if you have your own lecture notes on the topic from the days when you used to do nothing but lecture, let the group read them. Your main concern at this time is to make sure that the Authority Groups become authorities on their topics. They should know (as far as is possible) what you know about the topic. Expect high-quality presentations and you will get them. The responsibility of each Authority Group is to make sure that the students in their Presentation Group know (as far as is possible) what *they* know about the topic.

Allow plenty of time for the Authority Group to become authorities on their topic. Depending on the material, this might take up to three classroom periods. Students might need to go to the library for one of these periods to do research. (Because I will often have three different classes, 90 students in all, dealing with the same novel, I spare the librarians by photocopying relevant material — for example, reviews of a novel. My having copies of this material in the classroom saves students a trip to the library.) I seldom have to encourage students to work together on their own time; they quickly see the benefits of doing so.

6. If students are involved in the basic Jigsaw workshop in which each member of the Authority Group will be presenting alone within a Presentation Group, ask each member of the Authority Group to write a plan of her/his presentation and bring it to an upcoming meeting. This draft should contain all the relevant material that members of the group have discussed over the past few days, shaped and refined for presentation. It must also contain activities, workshops, even games in which each presenter will involve the students actively. The Authority Group should not prepare a set of lecture notes to read to their "students." That would be the antithesis of active learning.

7. Allow time so that each member presents his/her ideas to the Authority Group. As members will soon be making their own individual presentations for an uninformed audience, they will listen to the plans with care and possibly take a few notes to enhance their own presentation. If one member has prepared a particularly effective visual aid, game, quiz, roleplaying session, or other activity that will involve students actively, others may want to include it in their own presentation. Encourage cooperative learning.

8. As the presentations will begin soon, encourage each Authority Group to have a "dress rehearsal." Each member should present virtually the same material, but in his or her own style. Encourage presenters to stretch their imaginations during the presentation.

Each year students amaze me with new, innovative ways of presenting material while all the time remaining authorities on their topics. To involve their listeners, presenters use roleplaying techniques, board or TV-show games, video equipment, charts to be completed during the session, debates, etc. On occasion, the Authority Group may even decide to make a collective presentation for a few minutes before the class splits up into small groups. In summary, an Authority Group is fully responsible for its session.

Procedure for the Presentation Group

1. Re-arrange the class for Presentation Groups. The easiest method to do so is to have students sign their names within a grid. Names going down will be members of Authority Groups; names going across, members of Presentation Groups. Have the Grid posted on presentation days so all students know who is in each group. For example, jigsawing *The Mosquito Coast*:

TOPICS		Arche-types	Myths	Form	Symbol	Allusion	Societies	Setting	Author
S T U D E N T S	1	Bill	Joan	Ali	Sani	Ruth	Mai	George	Al
	2	Sing	Betty	Frank	Phil	Wooli	...	...	...
	3	John	Jackie	Surhan	Martha	...	...	...	...
	4	Dick	Suzy	Rusty	...	...	...	...	...

Note: This grid shows Bill, Sing, John, and Dick as presenters on their topic of "archetypes" within *The Mosquito Coast*. Bill will be presenting to Joan, Ali, Sani, and so on..

Each member of the Authority Group is now on his or her own with an uninformed audience of seven students. During the presentation, encourage listeners to interrupt and ask questions, argue points, ask for clarifications, embellish specific points if they know details about the topic, etc.

Hint: If one of the Authority Group members is absent, the students from his or her group can move to other Presentation Groups so that they do not miss the presentation. (For missing presenters, I assign a detailed, formal essay.)

2. If each presentation takes half an hour and you have eight different Authority Groups, you will be able to complete the presentations in four one-hour class periods.

3. During the presentations, make sure that the presenters are in corners or against the walls with their "students" facing them. You will be able to circulate from group to group – helping out if necessary. You can also indicate how much time each presenter has left by catching his/her eye.

4. If appropriate to the topic, ask students to prepare an essay or other project after their presentation. They will enter this part of their learning process with confidence, having prepared their material within an Authority Group, presented and discussed their material within a Presentation Group, and received an evaluation of their presentation by a group of their peers.

   For variety, you might ask all Authority Group members to make up essay topics or other suitable projects to assign to their Presentation Groups. Because students might receive up to seven projects, suggest that they choose only one or two to complete. Students should write the essay or complete the assignment and give it to their presenter to edit (and grade, if you wish).

5. After the completion of each presentation, I usually call the presenters together and have a discussion as to how *they* think their sessions went. They are usually quite excited by "teaching" their first active-learning lesson. Generally they wish they had more time – the classic statement of teachers. Finally, I ask them to fill in an Evaluation Form of their work within the Authority Group. (See Evaluation of Authority Group form in this chapter.)

6. While I talk with the Authority Group, the members of each Presentation Group evaluate the presenters and fill in an evaluation form on the effectiveness of the session. They might even assign a mark. (See Evaluation of Presentation form in this chapter.)

7. There are several ways to grade a Jigsaw workshop. You can ask each member of the Authority Group to submit an Evaluation Form with a mark out of 5, stapled on top of the Evaluation Forms from the "students" in the Presentation Group. You can check all of the marks, hoping that the mark each presenter assigns will be the same as those the "students" assign and the same as the one you will assign. Return the Evaluation Forms with your assigned mark and a comment.

   Alternatively, when you evaluate the Jigsaw workshop, you can decide to give a single, collective grade to the Authority Group so that they can share it among their members. For example, if you assign a 3 out of 5 and there are four members in the Authority Group, you would give them 12 marks. They would have to negotiate and assign marks to each member of the group. If they all worked equally, each would receive a 3.

There are a number of benefits to the Jigsaw workshop. Students often prepare interesting visuals for their presentations, consisting of pictures, diagrams, models, games, student essays, etc. If you have other classes, all engaged in similar Jigsaw workshops, students will be keenly interested in viewing these displays. They quite often will pick up additional ideas on a topic that they either presented or participated in. In addition, you might also conduct a class discussion on the displays. Student feedback will, no doubt, provide ideas for modifications that you might consider the next time you introduce the Jigsaw workshop. (See some variations below.) Finally, you might ask your students to prepare questions on the material that they worked on because they have not received adequate answers during the presentation. Students will be anxious to hear *your* answers to questions that have been troubling them. They will be active instead of passive listeners.

Group -Teach Jigsaw

Teacher Preparation: Look at the workshop "Group Teaching" in Chapter 7. Before you begin a unit of course content, divide the material into several manageable chunks. Assign students to each Authority Group to "teach" one portion of the course content.

Length of Time: Allow students no more than two class periods to prepare. They will probably find time out of class to get together to refine their presentation. Each presentation should take 15 minutes.

• Because Group-Teach Jigsaw workshops are less intimidating than the other Jigsaw workshops, I suggest that you introduce your students to jigsawing by assigning small groups of five or six students to teach, collectively, a portion of course content to the rest of the class within a 15-minute lesson. Ask students to sign their names in a grid under titles that interest them; for example, for a Math class — Adding Fractions, Subtracting Fractions, Multiplying Fractions, and Dividing Fractions; for science — one of the planets or one of a series of scientific experiments; and so on.

• During their presentation, they should designate one person to handle the background of the topic; another to handle the meaning and significance of the topic; another, to analyze; another, to help their "students" to apply their knowledge and understanding of the topic to other situations; and finally, all should engage in an evaluation of the products of the application.

• Take a few minutes to decide which units of course content you might use to Group Teach.

IDEAS FOR GROUP-TEACH JIGSAW WORKSHOPS

Desktop Teaching Jigsaw

- I suggest that the second time you introduce jigsawing to your students, you use "Desktop Teaching," already outlined in Chapter Seven. Although students can become authorities on their own topic and could theoretically teach it to the rest of the class, they usually only have to teach a small portion of a topic to one student at a time.

One-to-Three

- If you have only four important topics to deal with, assign the same topic to two different groups. Each group will work on the topic separately.

TOPICS	A	B	C	D		A	B	C	D
S T U D E N T S 1					5				
2					6				
3					7				
4					8				

- Read vertically for eight Authority Groupings working on four different topics; read horizontally for eight Presentation Groupings presenting to an audience of three.
- I often start with this variation of the basic Jigsaw because it is less intimidating for students as the audience is smaller.

Four-to-All

- This Jigsaw is handled similarly to the Group-Teach Jigsaw, except that the groups prepare more difficult material. Eight Authority Groups, with four students in each, prepare a different topic and present to the entire class.
- In this variation, students must divide the material among themselves within their Authority Group so that they do not duplicate each other's material during their presentation. This variation allows for a more elaborate presentation: slide show, dialogues, demonstrations, a video production, etc. They might even roleplay: students could assume the personæ of characters from a piece of literature, historical personalities, inanimate objects, etc. Students will receive a group mark for their presentation; in addition, you may require each group to write an essay (See "Collaborative Writing," Chapter 4).

One-on-One

- Each student becomes an Authority and must prepare to "teach" one other student something specific: a figure of speech, a term, a definition, etc. Presenters should attempt to involve their "students" actively, and may devise a visual product to make their session memorable.

- Depending on how many specific things you want students to learn, divide the class accordingly. For example, you may want them to know, understand, and appreciate eight different things. Count off students by 1,2,3,4,5,6,7,8; 1,2, etc. In a class of 32, you will have four presenters individually preparing a presentation on each topic. It will be each presenter's responsibility to teach it the next day to one student at a time with as many elaborate explanations, examples, and illustrations as he/she can come up with to involve them.
- During the presentation, the presenters should wear something to indicate their topic of authority. All students should seek out those authorities they need; for example, if they are shaky on a particular topic, they should find one of the four presenters who is an authority and ask for a presentation. Students should continue to circulate so that they constantly form different pairs: one teaching, the other learning. The "student teacher" may repeat his or her "lesson" many times during the presentation. If one student does not quite understand a concept, he/she can find another presenter on the same topic, who might use a different approach. As they repeat their presentations, students will become more and more proficient. You might like to combine this Jigsaw variation with "Food with Thought" (See Chapter 17).

Further Variations

- Once you begin using Jigsaw workshops, you will discover many other variations; for example, two Authorities present the "pros" on a particular topic to two students who will later present the "cons." Or, you might divide the class into groups of three. Each group might present a five-minute live or video presentation for the whole class on a particular topic (see "Synthesis" Chapter 22). Or groups of five might present short scenes they have written, based on course content. On a given day, the teacher can schedule the scenes.

A far better method of teaching than lecturing to a large group of passive listeners, the Jigsaw workshop allows students to become actively involved with the course content, to question and offer comments with confidence, to discover how the course content affects aspects of their own lives, to learn the benefits of cooperating within an active-learning environment, and to have a real sense of **owning** the course content.

Handouts to Authority Groups

- The main work you need to do for a Jigsaw workshop is to prepare handouts to each Authority Group on the different topics in order to help them become authorities on their topics.
- Although you want to encourage individual creativity among the members of the Authority Groups, you will want to ensure the quality and accuracy of their material. Nothing is gained by the uninformed leading the uninformed. Here is an example of one of several handouts that I would give to all members of one Authority Group to help them become authorities on the mythological links within Paul Theroux's *The Mosquito Coast*. (Other handouts focus on archetypal links, sociological links, psychoanalytical links, and so on.) The method of presentation rests with the Authority Group. The leader of the Authority Group should invite you to one of the preparation sessions (or you should just visit the group) in order to clarify, encourage, correct, modify, or offer additional help.

Mythological Links to The Mosquito Coast

Use the following information to become an authority on your topic. Remember when you present that you should involve your "students," not just have them sit passively and listen to you.

When you look for mythological links, search for the ways in which certain types of events, characters, situations, and conflicts touch deep chords in human nature. Based on communal beliefs, mythology is affiliated with religion, anthropology, and cultural history.

In addition to applying what you learned while watching the Joseph Campbell/Bill Moyers *Power of Myth* series and to reading the packet of available reviews of the novel, you might want to ask yourselves the following questions to help you compose your first journal entry:

Are there strong communal beliefs in the novel?
1. Belief in Supreme Being(s): creator, judge, prime mover, religion, fate
2. Belief in power of nature: Mother Nature, natural disasters, magical places (holy wells, sacred rocks)

Think of Allie as a prime mover (a god). Deal with the religious conflicts between Allie and Spellgood. Link Mother and Mother Nature. Deal with the Acre as a holy place. Deal with Fat Boy as Allie.

Does Theroux use any images in the novel?
1. Water: birth, death, resurrection; life cycle; eternity
2. Colors
   red: blood, sacrifice, violence
   green: hope, fertility, death, decay
   black: the unknown, death, evil
   blue: virginal, Mary
3. Numbers
   Three: spiritual unity, male
   Four: life cycle, seasons, elements, female
   Seven: powerful because it unites three and four, perfect
4. Garden: paradise, innocence, unspoiled beauty
5. Tree: immortality, inexhaustible life

What is the image of Fat Boy, the Acre, the Three Men, upriver, the scarecrow, Jeronimo? Link Fat Boy to the first two atom bombs: Fat Man and Little Boy. Link the film *Fat Man and Little Boy* to *The Mosquito Coast* and mythology.

What motifs are in the novel? Remember, a motif recurs.
1. Creation   2. Immortality
   In what ways is Allie like a god? In what ways is he not? Deal with Birth, Death, and Resurrection in the novel. How are Allie and Prometheus similar? (Remember that Prometheus gave humanity fire.)

In ten words, what is the theme of *The Mosquito Coast*?

How is the story of Allie Fox mythic? What sort of legends can you see developing in Honduras after Allie's death? What makes a myth memorable?

How is the story of Allie Fox epic? Examine epic poetry. What kind of a person is an epic hero? Try your hand at writing an epic poem with Allie Fox as hero.

Don't forget to make up an essay question on your topic which you can give to the members of your Presentation Group.

- Remember, all of the other Authority Groups will receive their own, different handout to help them become authorities on their specific topics.

IDEAS FOR YOUR OWN HANDOUTS TO AUTHORITY GROUPS

Evaluations

- To help students improve the Jigsaw, ask them to complete the evaluation forms on the next two pages. You may adapt the forms to fit your needs, make up your own, or, better still, make up forms **with** your students.
- While you are talking to the presenters after the jigsaw, the others should complete the evaluation of the presentation. When they are finished, they should give their form to their presenter. Later, each presenter can complete his/her evaluation form of the Authority Group, staple the presentation evaluations together, and hand the packet to you for your evaluation.

Evaluation of Presentation   Date of Presentation _____

Topic: _____

Presenter: _____ Evaluator:_____

After your presenter has finished, evaluate the presentation. Put a checkmark on each line to reflect your evaluation; a check mark on the right indicates good work; on the left, poor work. Also, feel free to elaborate in detail on the back so that you justify the position of any checkmark you placed on the extreme right or left. Remember, the purpose of this evaluation is to help the presenter improve.

Content and Organization

unclear ideas.. clear thesis
little knowledge................................... thorough knowledge
support unclear..................................... worthwhile support
surface treatment... complete
no conclusion.................................... effective summary

Delivery

hesitant...confident
little or no eye contact............................effective eye contact
poor rapport with group............................effective rapport
hard to understand............................. easy to understand
inaudible, too fast/slow........................... good pace, volume

Strategies

poor outline for notes........................ skeletal outline helpful
no discussion.................................... good discussion
provided no visual aids........................ excellent use of visuals

Overall Impression

boring..exciting
little help... very helpful
careless... careful
little preparation............................. diligent preparation

What did you like best about the presentation?_____

_____

_____

What should the presenter work on before the next presentation?

_____

_____

If you had to give a mark out of 5 to the presenter, what would you give? ___
Justify your decision.

_____

_____

_____

Evaluation of Authority Group   Date _____

Topic _____ Presenter _____

What did you learn from the other members of your Authority Group?

_____

_____

_____

Who from your Authority Group helped you most?_____

What did you like best about working with your Authority Group?

_____

_____

_____

What changes would have made the Authority Group even better?

_____

_____

_____

What were you most pleased with during your presentation?

_____

_____

_____

What would you change if you had a chance to repeat your presentation?

_____

_____

_____

If you had to give yourself a mark out of 5 for your contribution to your Authority Group and your "teaching" in the Presentation Group, what would you give? ___

Justify your mark.

_____

_____

_____

_____

_____

_____

_____

YOUR OWN IDEAS FOR JIGSAWING

CHAPTER TWELVE

Student Publications and Productions

Publication of students' work helps students make their school work real, but it also publicizes to a large, real audience what students are capable of achieving. Too many times we hide our students' lights under bushels. Newsletters, Newspapers, Productions, Open Houses, Traditions, Anthologies, and Videos are only a few ways that you can make school projects beneficial for students and others. Adapt any of the following suggestions to fit your needs.

Weekly/Monthly Newspaper

Teacher Preparation: After reading the ideas below, decide whether you would like your students to have a class newspaper. If so, have a discussion with your students at the beginning of the term.

- Depending on your and their interest, you might like to have your students produce a weekly or monthly newspaper to reflect what has happened, what is happening, and what will happen within their classroom learning community. Divide small groups of students into the number of editions you wish to publish, each group being responsible for one edition. Have each group appoint an editor. Let the editors know the publication dates. It will be the editors' responsibility to collect the articles written by the other members in their group, type the material, arrange for art work, and provide you with final copy for publication just prior to the publication date. Because you do not have time to get any part of the newspaper ready, let the editors know that the material you receive *must* be photocopy-ready, so that all you need do is have it duplicated. In some cases, however, an industrious group will duplicate their publication themselves.
- At the beginning of the term, you may collectively decide on a name for your class newspaper, but from then on each group should be on its own to collect material and write columns that have a direct bearing on the content of your course. You might also choose to write a short column if you wish. If possible, choose very reliable students as your first group; they will set the tone and style of the paper. Even so, you will doubtless see an improvement in the quality of newspapers as the term continues.
- If you ask your students to take on this project, you will probably want to provide them with several ideas about content. My English Lit weekly class newspaper has included regular columns dealing with course content: films, poetry, and novels. Some issues have also contained a film review; an announcement of the latest novel by the author of the one we are studying; original poetry; announcements of TV shows that will be of interest to the class; reviews of TV shows; letters to the editor; cartoons; comic strips;

details about contests sponsored by radio programs or magazines looking for original short stories, poems, and essays; list of due dates for term papers or exams; hints for studying. Each newspaper also lists the next editor's name and writers' names and any special requests for material that *they* are hoping to include in their edition.

- Students eagerly await a copy of their class newspaper each Monday (or the first of each month). They use parts of it as a guide to the week's (month's) work.
- If you wish to give marks to the editors and contributors, you might assign a token grade for each newspaper at the end of the term. Or you might have the students as a whole rank all editions and let your marks reflect their evaluation.

Anthologies

Teacher Preparation: After reading the material below, decide whether you think your class's creating an anthology is a good idea; if so, discuss strategies with your class.

- To encourage students to write for a real audience, you might like to announce that a particular assignment will be destined for publication in a class anthology. Once students have completed all of the assignments, you can appoint two or three students to place all of the assignments in a large, bound volume and submit it to the intended audience. They may choose to illustrate some of the pages and design the cover.
- You might consider, for example, that your students write poems for a children's hospital, short stories for a seniors' home, argumentative essays for a local library, lab reports for an upcoming science class, a Who's Who of historical figures for a reference book in the classroom, a book of recipes to sell to the public, etc.

IDEAS FOR PUBLICATIONS

Putting on a Show

- The best way for students to work with a play script is to involve them in a full-scale production. This, however, might be impossible for a number of reasons. But you can still dramatize the play instead of leaving the words on the printed page. Remember that plays were written to be performed, not studied in classrooms.
- The following workshops focus on individual scenes from a full-length play and will allow you and your students to painlessly produce several scenes.
- As an alternative to staging scenes in the classroom, you might suggest to your students that they videotape them in an appropriate setting. The "Video Productions" workshop in this chapter will give you ideas to help students put their work on tape.
- Consider using the next three workshops across the curriculum by producing plays and videos dealing with science, history, psychology, etc. For example, look at *RUR* by Karl Capek (science), *The Crucible* by Arthur Miller (history), *The Physicists* by Frederick Durrenmatt (science), or *The Good Woman of Sichuan* by Berthold Brecht (psychology).

A Roomful of Assistant Directors

Teacher Preparation: Choose a scene and a group of students to act out the roles in that scene. Students should come to class knowing the lines as well as possible; they don't need to memorize them.

Classroom Preparation: Provide an improvised setting. You might like to draw a groundview of the set on the chalkboard so that you can explain entrances and exits and various set pieces.

Length of Time: Depending on the length of the scene, from 10 to 30 minutes.

- Place your actors where you want them for the opening of the scene. Ask the rest of the class to serve as your assistant directors, making suggestions while you direct the actors. If you suggest that an actor move to a chair on a given line and the actor does it, you might ask your assistant directors if the actor could deliver the line in another way or move on a different line. After an assistant director makes a suggestion, have the actor execute it. You can then ask for a consensus of which way worked better.
- Continue to direct the rest of the scene in this way. Afterwards, have a complete runthrough of the scene and a follow-up discussion before working through another important scene from the play.
- By putting the characters of a play "on their feet," you and your class of assistant directors will more easily be able to read between the lines, unearth subtle interpretations, and arrive at deeper meanings.
- As a rule of thumb, actors and directors should study the dialogue with the following ideas in mind:
  - what a character says may not always be the truth
  - what a character does is generally the truth
  - what another character says *to* a character may not always be true
  - what another character says *about* an absent character is generally true (unless you know the speaker is dishonest)
  - what the playwright says *about* the character is true

Student Directors

Teacher Preparation: Decide which scenes you wish to present.
Length of Time: Spread rehearsals over several periods, but plan other
   activities as well. For presentations, about 5 minutes per scene.

- Divide the class into groups of 3, 4, 5, and 6, according to the number of characters in different scenes from the full-length play you're studying. Have each group choose a director, who in turn will choose a scene (2 or 3 pages) with the number of characters that corresponds with the number of "actors" in the group. You will therefore end up with scenes involving two, three, four, and five characters. Ask the directors to report to you when they have chosen their scenes so that you can record them. If two directors want to do the same scene, allow them to do so. Audiences enjoy seeing the same scenes with different actors and interpretations.
- Encourage lots of rehearsal, both in and out of school. Expect an invitation to rehearsals so that you can make suggestions.
- Conduct a dress rehearsal. Actors should not only be off book (know all their lines) for this performance but be in costume and makeup (improvised if necessary). Don't worry too much about the set; a few set pieces should satisfy all directors.
- For "opening night," you can produce the scenes in the order in which they appear in the original play. You might be the MC and bridge some of the scenes with a few explanatory notes so that the audience doesn't get lost. Then sit back and await the applause that you and your "performers" will surely receive.
- If the scenes prove very popular, you might want to consider producing them, or perhaps even the entire play, in front of several classes, the entire school, or the community. If your class decides a larger production might be successful, they will have to arrange for a larger space to hold both performers and audience, the printing of programs and methods of advertising, perhaps more elaborate sets and costumes, and make other preparations for their new audience and purpose. Who knows? This might be just the inspiration your school needs to form a drama club, if one doesn't exist there.

Video Productions

Teacher Preparation: After reading the material below, decide on your
   involvement in video productions. Discuss the details with your class.

- Divide the class into groups of five or six. Have them appoint a director who will involve the other members of the group in making a video production. The production can take many forms: a commercial on ecology, a filmed poem, a dramatization of a scientific experiment, a lesson on a problem-solving technique, a rock video on how to learn something, any "how-to" video, or a filming of the scenes from the previous workshop.
- Once they have completed their videos, the groups can show them to the rest of the class for evaluation. Then, as a group, decide on an audience that would appreciate seeing them: children's hospital, seniors' home, another class, a government department, etc.
- Chances are that more than one student in your class has experience that other students will find useful in preparing and shooting a video. You might want

to encourage students without any experience to conduct a treasure hunt (see "Inviting the Expert," Chapter Ten) for classmates who have filmed or appeared in videos, done sound recording (as a member of a band, for example), worked with makeup in theatre or modeling, or have other skills that beginners in video production might find useful.

- To help students learn the nitty-gritty of video production, you might ask someone from your school district's audio-visual department to guide students in the use of a camcorder. You might also want to duplicate the following information, adapting it as you see fit.

Tips for Video Production

Pre-production

The best way to guarantee a high-quality video production is to plan it carefully. In video, planning is called pre-production. Professional video producers often spend more time on pre-production than they spend on the production session itself. Thorough pre-production saves both time and money, and also results in a higher quality video program. You will save yourself hours of anxiety if you are totally prepared before you actually film your video program with actors, props, setting, camera, sound and lighting equipment, and crew.

To help you become familiar with some of the terms used in video production, we will be conducting a Desktop Teaching workshop*, using the following terms:

aperture, artificial light, audio dub, audio track, back light, camera operator, cassette, close-up, crew, crop, cue, director, editing, establishing shot, extreme close-up, fade, fill light, frame, framing, freeze frame (still frame), F-stops, glitch, graphics, high-angle shot, image, in-camera editing, iris, key light, lens, lens barrel, long shot, low-angle shot, master tape, medium shot, normal-angle shot, pan, producer, scenario, scene, script, shot, special effects, standby, storyboard, subject, tilt, titles, transition, videotape, zoom.

Notes to the Producer
- During pre-production you first determine your variables. What do you want to film (topic), why do you want to make a video (purpose), who do you want to see it (audience), and what kind of a video do you want to make (format)?
- Finding a script or having one especially composed is an essential pre-production duty of all producers. If you are not writing the script yourself, make sure that you give specific instructions to your writers so that they come up with one that suits you and fulfils your purpose.
- While the script is being written, you need to select shooting locations, find or build props and scenery, choose on-camera performers and a shooting crew, draw up a schedule for rehearsals and shooting sessions, make a list of all equipment and supplies you will need, and plan and prepare any graphics or artwork that you will want to use.
- As the producer, you must organize your production team so that everyone is working toward the day of the shoot, when filming takes place. The producer should keep tabs on the team to make sure that no one gets behind.
- Give your production team a rehearsal and shooting schedule. You might adapt the following one to fit your needs:

⇨

---

* Chapter 7

Rehearsal and Shooting Schedule

Producer's Name _____

Name of Production _____

Rehearsal Times _____ _____ _____ _____

Date of Shooting Session _____

Location of Shooting Session_____

Director's Name _____

Performers' Names   Performers' Roles

_____   _____

_____   _____

_____   _____

Crew: Camera Operator _____

          Sound Operator _____

Equipment Needed (Mark Yes or No for each item as you pack for shooting)

_____ video camera

_____ camera tripod

_____ extension camera cable

_____ VTR portable deck

_____ TV set for playback

_____ blank cassettes

_____ charged batteries

_____ spare battery

_____ AC adapter/battery charger

_____ additional lights

_____ electrical extension cords

_____ external microphone

_____ earphone or headphones (for monitoring sound as you record)

_____ tape recorder/record player

_____ music (tape/record)

_____ sound effects

_____ scripts

_____ clipboard

_____ paper and pencils

_____ duct tape (for securing microphone and camera cables)

_____ graphics/titles/pictures/art work

_____ sets (specify)_____

_____ furniture/furnishings (specify) _____

_____

_____ props (specify)_____

_____

_____ costumes (specify) _____

_____

_____ make-up (specify) _____

_____

_____ other (specify) _____

_____

- You as producer must complete all of the preparation before the day of the shoot. Therefore, you will need to try one of the three basic methods of writing and arranging a video shooting session depending on your format: shooting scenario, script, or storyboard. A shooting scenario is the easiest to use, so it will probably work best for inexperienced performers. Consult a textbook on video production for details about scripts and storyboards.

  Shooting scenarios are especially good for organizing documentaries and interviews. They are also good if you do not care about precise timing and are not depending on your "performers" to memorize exact lines. Basically, a shooting scenario is a rough outline that tells the camera operators where to set up their cameras and what kind of shots to take, the on-camera performers where they should be, the crew how to arrange the props and furnishings, and the director the order of each shot.

- Once the producer has established the location, he/she should make up a shooting scenario, carefully noting everything that might affect the production: position of windows, electrical outlets, available furniture, colors of background, size of space, best location to shoot the video, etc.

- Spend a few minutes studying the following excerpt from a shooting scenario.

Production Title: How Cold is Cold? A Look at Dry Ice
Producer: Susanna Chung
Location: Chemistry Lab
    Laurier Sr. Secondary
Date: Wed, Oct. 1, 11:00
Estimated Length of Program: 10 minutes

Shot No.	Content of Shot	Time of shot	Notes
1	CU of block of ice	5 seconds	Camera on tripod about 3 metres in front of lab table
	Pan to block of dry ice – close to black	10 seconds	Block of ice on paper towel on table – block of dry ice on pad on table next to regular ice
2	Open from black to Card 1 "How Cold is Cold?" Flip card down to Card 2 "A Look at Dry Ice"	15 seconds	Cards on easel to R of table
3	Flip card down to Card 3 "with James Nguyen" Pan up to James behind lab table	20 seconds	Standing light 1 metre behind James's shoulder to light table. James (wearing lab coat and protective gloves): "Welcome to Chemistry 10. Today's show is for those of you who want to be really cool."

cont.

Note: a shooting scenario does not dictate exactly what the final video will look like; rather, it allows the producer, director, performers, camera operator, and crew members room to improvise as they shoot.

- Once you have completed your pre-production work, you might want to have one or two rehearsals before you film your production. If, for example, you have a number of performers in your video, you might like to have the director rehearse them without the crew until they are comfortable with their roles.

Production

Using all of your carefully thought-out pre-production plans, you should produce a satisfactory video. But be prepared for new things to happen. One shot may take ten seconds more than you planned. An actor may take less time to say a line than you anticipated. The weather may not cooperate for an outdoor shot and you will have to move indoors or under cover. Improvising on the spot can sometimes add an excitement to a video production that will make it even better. Do not worry about a scene that does not work. All you have to do is shoot a new scene (if you are going to piece together the best of several shots) or rewind the tape and reshoot the shot (if you are shooting the video in sequence and do not want to edit). The only thing that you will have to be concerned about in redoing a shot are the glitches. Play back your tape after you have filmed each shot to ensure it is free of glitches.

If you are uneasy about depending on your own wits, pick up one of the many texts on how to make a video from your local library.

After Production

Once you have your video edited and "in the can," show it to your class for their comments before you present it to your intended audience.

Because most of your classmates are probably authorities on watching video productions, they will easily let you know if they think yours works well or not. In all likelihood, since this is your first video and perhaps your equipment is not the best, you will be unhappy with some parts of your production. Perhaps you might start the evaluation session by thanking your performers and crew, explaining your viewing variables, sharing your concept of what you wanted your video to be like, and relating where you had to compromise your plans and settle for second or third best. Do not blame anyone for anything that did not come up to your expectations. Everyone probably tried his or her best to make your video production a hit. (Maybe your next one will earn you an Emmy!)

IDEAS FOR PRODUCTIONS

Traditions

Teacher Preparation: If your school has no or few traditions, you might like to consider establishing a few. After reading the ideas below, discuss the possibilities of establishing traditions in your school with the rest of your colleagues.

USSR

Teacher Preparation: If your school does not have an Uninterrupted Sustained Silent Reading program in which everyone in the school (principal, teachers, students, maintenance staff, etc.) stops whatever they are doing and reads non-stop for 20 minutes, you might consider establishing such a tradition in your school.
Length of Time: 20 minutes at the same time each day.

- All participants in USSR may bring anything they want to read. No one is allowed to write or speak. For 20 minutes, the entire school is given over to silent reading.

Epic Day

- On a visit to Catlin School in Portland, Oregon, I was delighted to see that the school community has established several traditions. Everyone in Catlin knows that the first Monday in November is EPIC DAY and that they can ask any tenth grader to recite his or her original epic. If you are ever present on the first Monday in November, you will see the principal, teachers, school nurse, visiting parents, and students from all other grades corner every tenth grader before school, during class breaks, lunch time, or after school and ask to hear his/her epic poem. Because of the tradition, ninth graders know what is in store for them in the tenth grade and over the summer start to bone up on epic poetry. Ninth graders, by the way, must participate in a Gilbert and Sullivan musical each year and eighth graders must learn twenty lines of Shakespeare and be ready to recite them to anyone who asks on SHAKESPEARE DAY.
- If you wish to start EPIC DAY at your school, find out how much your students already know about epics. Then, fill in for them the characteristics of epics. Next, have them read one. Once you feel they know and understand epic poetry, suggest that they choose a historical or living personality and write their own epic.
- On the following page is a set of instructions based on those Bob Ash from Catlin gives his students.

IDEAS FOR TRADITIONS FOR YOUR SCHOOL

Epic Day

1. Epics must be a minimum of 250 lines, maximum of 350. Number each 10 lines at the side.
2. The epic must be prepared on a word processor or typed and must be double spaced.
3. 100 lines must alliterate across the caesura. Each line will be marked thus * (see below).
4. An additional 25 lines must have all four beats alliterating and be marked **.
5. Remember that there is *no* rhyme.
6. All normal rules of punctuation apply with the sole exception that each new line will begin with a capital letter. Use plenty of enjambment.
7. Each line will have four stressed syllables. You should be able to mark each with a stress mark over the accented syllable, e.g., **úsual   todáy   begín   comméncement   respónd   desért   dessért**
8. Epic conventions: epic hero, a conflict or quest, worthy opponent, epic battle, begin *in medias res*, attention-getter at the beginning. ALL ARE NEEDED.
9. At least three allusions must be included and marked: Biblical allusion (BA), classical allusion (CA), literary allusion (LA).
10. Due Dates. It is very important that you do not miss *any* of these deadlines:

Mon. Sep. 26	1st ten lines due	Mon. Oct. 24	1st 250 lines
Mon. Oct. 3	1st 50 lines	Mon. Nov. 7	EPIC DAY You
Mon. Oct. 10	1st 125 lines		recite your epic to anyone you meet.

```
 *        Listen you sophomores, who labor each year
 * *      At puzzling out, planning and plotting the complexities
 *        Of an epic which will add to the aura of Catlin
 *        And its academic excellence.  Act now and begin
 *        A literary tour-de-force to extend your creativity
 *        In addition to your vocabulary.
                             Now the date has arrived
 *        When you have to put your ideas down on paper
 *        With lots of alliteration, enjambment and allusions,
 *        Go at it now with confidence and gusto,
CA *      Not like Damocles but eager and diligent,
 *        With thesaurus in hand and word processor humming,
 *        And compose two fifty lines to delight and enchant me.
```

• Ideas you might consider as traditions for your school:
 – Trial Day (for seniors): one day each year put someone on trial. (See Chapter Ten for details.)
 – Times Table Day (for a lower elementary grade): every student in that grade must recite, on request, any times table.
 – Experiment Day (for science students of any grade): on request, every student must involve another student in performing an experiment.
 – Physical Education Day (for PE students of any grade): from a set of exercises or physical feats that students compile, they must, on request, perform one exercise or feat.
 – Home Economics Day: students must sell something that they have baked (good for building up the school fund).

CHAPTER THIRTEEN

Problem-Solving Workshops

Presenting a group of five or six students with a problem that they have to solve within a limited time encourages higher-level thinking. Giving students an opportunity to solve not only course-content problems but also personal problems surely prepares them for situations they will face in the future.

To make a problem-solving group productive and help it function smoothly, encourage students to brainstorm fully and ask each one to perform one of the following tasks:

Leader	who keeps the group on track, making sure that they are addressing the problem, occasionally asking someone to summarize or restate the problem and what others have said
Observer	who sees to it that everyone participates and has an opportunity to speak, instead of allowing anyone to monopolize
Time Keeper	who keeps track of time, making sure that the recorder has enough time to record all possible solutions
Recorder	who writes down the best solutions of the group and reports them to you and the rest of the class during a class discussion

Without getting too involved in the theory with your students, you might like to plunge into a few simple workshops in which you prove to them that "None of us is as smart as *all* of us." Later in the term, you can introduce students to deductive and inductive reasoning, higher-level thinking strategies, and provocative or divergent questioning.

Squares

Teacher Preparation: Duplicate the diagram on the next page on an overhead transparency. To add to the difficulty of the problem, you might add eight more lines to divide each small square into four more squares.

Length of Time: 3 minutes for individual solutions; 5 minutes for group solutions.

- Ask students, "How many complete squares can you find?" Students should work alone.

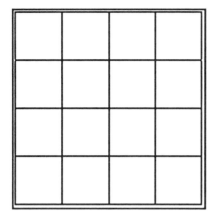

- After three minutes of individual solving, ask students to form groups of three or four. Ask them if they are all in agreement about how many squares the figure contains. If they are not, the one who found the most squares will doubtless show the others how he/she found them. They should work quietly so that other groups do not overhear their solutions. Once all the groups have reached a consensus, check how many squares each group found. If one group found more than the others, have that group's leader go to the overhead projector and show the rest of the class all the squares.
- You can do the same workshop with triangles, rectangles, or circles.

Note: The next three workshops deal with theories that will lead students to critical thinking and empower them to solve problems. I have demonstrated each with questions from *The Unbearable Lightness of Being* by Milan Kundera. As you go through each, adapt the questions to fit your own course content, grade and subject.

Reflective Questioning

> *Teacher Preparation*: After reading over the information below, prepare some reflective questions to help your students understand the importance of being a risk taker in asking questions which will lead to critical thinking.
>
> *Length of Time*: One class period.

- This workshop is designed to encourage students to take risks and reflect on problems in original, flexible, elaborate, and intelligent ways.
  - **Forced-Association Questions** force students to compare diverse ideas and elements with other ideas. For example, after Jigsawing *The Unbearable Lightness of Being*, I asked, "*What* was life like in Prague in 1968? *How* does it compare with life in Prague today?" After hearing several answers and allowing plenty of discussion on questions you compose, you can ask students to make up other Forced-Association Questions and, in small groups, pose their "What...How" questions to other members of their group.
  - **Quantity Questions** encourage elaborate thought. For example, I asked, "*If* Kundera wanted to set his story in Beijing in 1989 instead of in Prague in 1968, *what* are all the things he'd have to change?" After discussion of your questions, you can encourage students to make up other "If...what" questions.

–**Viewpoint Questions** encourage students to see things from different points of view. For example, "*How would* Margaret Atwood write the story of Tomas and Tereza?" Later, encourage students to make up "How would" questions similar to those you have posed.

–**Reorganization Questions** encourage creative and flexible approaches to the present and future. For example, "*Suppose* Tomas and Tereza did not produce a son (as in the movie version). *What would be the consequences* of the storyline?" Later, encourage students to make up "Suppose...what would be the consequences" questions similar to yours.

Deductive Thinking

Teacher Preparation: After reading over the information below, make up sample questions to help students understand the importance of deductive reasoning.

Length of Time: One class period to begin with; then, as often as you wish.

• This workshop encourages students to move from the general to the specific and link facts and general rules to reach a deductive conclusion. It also empowers students to make up general statements that must be supported with specific facts.

• After Jigsawing *The Unbearable Lightness of Being* with my students, I posed several general interpretive statements to my class as a whole and, in discussion, asked them to support the major premise in order to formulate conclusions that they are happy with. For example, "Thomas and Tereza die happy." or "Kundera's setting (Prague 1968) affects his main four characters' lives." Using the statements you have composed as examples, encourage students to pose their own general interpretive statements within groups and ask them to support their major premise.

Inductive Thinking

Teacher Preparation: After reading over the information below, make up a sample activity to help students understand the importance of inductive reasoning.

Length of Time: One class period to begin with; then, as often as you wish.

• This workshop encourages students to move from several specific statements and a great deal of data to a *probable* generalization that begins with something like, "Most of the time..." or "Most people..." or "If you do this, you will probably get..." rather than "All people will..." or "Every time you do this you will get..."

• You might like to introduce inductive thinking before you start a unit of course content, to determine how much students already know. You will have them brainstorm, categorize, set up a matrix, and find a generalization. While engaged in inductive reasoning with your class, you can help develop their thinking processes by asking leading questions. Thus, you can combine active learning and lecturing to teach course content.

• Using *The Unbearable Lightness of Being* as course content for inductive thinking, I asked my students to brainstorm the novel, looking for specific information dealing with Tomas's philosophy of love. They came up with several examples of Tomas's lovemaking (he's a regular womanizer at the beginning of the novel) and the fact that he separates being in love and lovemaking. Then, I asked the students to categorize the data to make it useful. Quickly they made a graphic – a table with two columns – labelling one "Lovemaking" and the other "Being in Love." After they grouped their data in a useful form, they set up an appropriate matrix so that they saw patterns forming. For example, looking at Tomas's movement from the beginning to the end of the novel:

Where is Tomas?	with Whom?	Results	What does reader learn?
in Prague			
in country			
in Prague again			
in Geneva			
in Prague again			
in country again			

- As students complete the matrix, they discover inferences so that they quite naturally find a generalization by looking down and across the columns of the matrix. For example, from using all of the specific data from the text, students will see that Tomas has learned to merge lovemaking and being in love rather than treating them as two separate functions.
- Make up a problem along the same lines to generate inductive thinking for your grade and subject. To help you think of a suitable one, look at the Senses Grid and Partial Grid in Chapter Eight.

Low- and High-Level Thinking

Teacher Preparation: After you have looked at Section Three of this book, you can focus on problem solving from another point of view.
Length of Time: One class period to review the taxonomy.

- This workshop encourages students to move from low-level thinking (knowledge and comprehension) to high-level thinking (analysis, application, evaluation, and synthesis). By encouraging students to make up low- and high-level questions, this workshop empowers students to note the difference between knowing and understanding "just the facts" and analyzing, applying, evaluating, and synthesizing the learned material.

- After demonstrating questioning techniques through the whole range of thinking strategies, I encourage students to make up their own questions (using the key words found in each chapter in Section Three). For example, here are six Low- and High-Level Questions based on *The Unbearable Lightness of Being*:
    - Knowledge: "Who are the Tristan and Don Juan referred to in the line 'Tomas died as Tristan, not as Don Juan' (124)"?
    - Comprehension: "Why does Sabina allude to Tristan and Don Juan when she is thinking about Tomas?"
    - Analysis: "Point out how Tomas is first a Don Juan and then a Tristan."
    - Application: "Assume that Tereza is reflecting on Tomas' death. To whom would *she* compare him?"
    - Evaluation: "Determine Tereza's and Sabina's estimation of Tomas."
    - Synthesis: "Hypothesize that you are Tomas. How do you think someone close to you would fill in the blanks of '_____ [your name] died as _____, not as _____.' How would you, yourself, fill in the blanks? Why not give someone close to you an opportunity to demonstrate how you have changed by asking him/her to fill in the blanks?"

Why?

Teacher Preparation: Using either a body of course-related material or personal, social, or political issues that you think important for your classes, make up a few "Why?" problems.
Length of Time: A few minutes each day.

- Within a full class or in small groups, pose "Why?" problems for students to solve. For example, "Why did Kundera write *The Unbearable Lightness of Being*?" Because there is no right answer to this question, students will have to offer a variety of possible answers and then evaluate them to determine the best. After asking them to solve your "Why?" problems, encourage students to pose their own "Why?" questions either within a full-class discussion or in small-group sessions.
- In order to arrive at adequate solutions, encourage students to use a variety of techniques (Reflective Thinking, Deductive and Inductive Thinking, Roleplaying, and Low- and High-Level Thinking) while they compose and solve "Why?" problems.

What Would Happen If...?

Teacher Preparation: Pose a few hypothetical problems to encourage creative problem solving.
Length of Time: 10 to 15 minutes for each problem.

- After completing a unit of material, pose a "What would happen if...?" question to test students' knowledge and understanding of the course content and also their ability to synthesize it. For example, in geography class: "What would happen if the ice age returned?" or "What would happen in North America if all the land west of the San Andreas Fault fell into the Pacific?" Or in a history class, after students have studied the Second World War, "What would happen if Hitler had won the war?"

- If you are interested in having students develop self-reflective thinking, pose social "What would happen if..." questions, such as "What would happen if a vaccine for AIDS were found tomorrow?" or "What would happen if you reversed roles with___?" This last question lends itself nicely to roleplaying activities.

Roleplaying

Teacher Preparation: Ask for volunteers and establish a scenario.
Length of Time: 4 or 5 minutes each.

- Explain to students that they do not have to be great actors in order to be successful roleplayers; they only need to be able to put themselves in someone else's place and imagine how that person would feel and respond. If some students are uncomfortable roleplaying in front of the rest of the class, have them all pair up and everyone in the class roleplay at the same time. This process involves everyone in the class, so there is no audience.
- Use the following information either for a single roleplaying session in front of the entire class or many simultaneous roleplaying sessions.
- Establish a scenario. For example, if you are studying the Civil War, set up three chairs. Three students should sit down. Try to have a mixture of sexes. Establish that the scene involves a mother and father and a son or daughter (depending on the third student). Say to the group(s), "You are a mother named _____(ask student(s) to give a name) and you are a father named _____. Your son (daughter), named _____, comes to see you with a problem. He/she has been invited to a party and will be going with someone who is green. The mother doesn't mind; she likes green people. But the father hates green people and will not allow his child to go on the date. Resolve the problem."
- Then, let the three go to it. If the whole class is in groups of three, the session will get quite heated, but be a lot of fun. If you have only three presenting at the front of the room, you can use various techniques to foster deeper thinking. You may ask them to "Freeze" and provide clarifications or an additional problem.
- On occasion, you might like to give each performer a coach. The coaches sit near the performers, but with their backs to the audience; their purpose is to provide ideas for their performers to help bring the problem to a conclusion. For variety, you might reverse roles: Mother can now be against and the Father for; a coach can become a performer; the Son can change with the Father; etc. When you feel that the roleplaying session has fulfilled your purpose, you can end it and have a discussion. During the discussion, you can have students link the roleplaying with the historical events, pointing out the similarities and differences.

Hint: I prefer total active involvement; therefore, I seldom will have only one roleplaying session. After an entire class has participated in the same roleplaying session, we will have a much richer class discussion because everyone has experienced the event. From time to time, because of observing one particularly successful roleplaying session, I might ask the group to present theirs for the rest of the class.

- By introducing roleplaying sessions into the class, you will encourage students to use roleplaying in workshops they will conduct. For example, a group of students presented a post-viewing workshop on the film *Battleship Potemkin*. They divided the class into pairs. They gave one member of each pair a list of characteristics of Eisenstein, the director of the film, and a list of statements of his beliefs and theories as they pertained to his film. To the other member of each pair, they gave a list of characteristics of an interrogator from the Czarist regime with a list of hard-line questions. For five minutes the entire class was involved in an interrogation roleplaying scene. Afterwards, the group leaders asked, "Who won: Eisenstein or the interrogator?" A good discussion followed.

Personal Problem-Solving

Teacher Preparation: Duplicate a current newspaper article that contains a problem that you think will interest your students and for which they can offer a choice of solutions. If you wish, use the one below.

Length of Time: 30 minutes plus a feedback session.

Spotlight on Youth
Battling a 'frightening' drop-out rate

by Andrew Hanon

Fourteen-year-old Dave hates school. Everybody, his parents, teachers and friends, know he would rather be anywhere than in class.

The only reason he even bothers to show up most days is because his buddies are there. While the lessons bore him beyond belief, at least he can while away the time at the back of the class with the guys, swapping crude jokes, whistling at girls and doing their best to drive the teachers crazy.

Once school is out for the day, Dave and his buddies head for the park, where they might smoke a little weed, or just hang out at the local convenience store, often until well past midnight. That's where the action is.

Sometimes as many as 100 kids gather in the store's parking lot, where they just goof around. Once in a while, if he has any money, Dave will score some dope from one of the many youths who deal. Occasionally a fight breaks out or the store's manager will call the police, but things are usually pretty calm.

His parents are pulling out their hair trying to get Dave to stay home on weeknights so he can at least attempt to do some homework. He is failing all his classes, and if something isn't done soon he will have to repeat the eighth grade a second time.

Time is running out, and Dave's teachers know it. If something isn't done soon to rekindle his interest in school, he will drop out with nothing more than a grade seven education, which in today's job market gives him little chance of ever making a life for himself....

- Problem to be solved: How would you keep Dave in school?
- Let student groups decide on the procedure they will follow to solve the problem:
    - Assigning roles – teacher, counsellor, principal, parent, Dave, shop-keeper, police, fellow student
    - Assigning duties – recorder, time keeper, observer, leader
- Let students decide on the techniques (Reflective Thinking, Deductive and Inductive Thinking, Low- and High-Level Thinking, Roleplaying) to use to solve the problem.

- The group attempts to reach a consensus and report to the teacher and the rest of the class.
- Besides giving students newspaper articles, you might think of some problems, or better still, ask students to write anonymous suggestions on pieces of paper and drop them into a box. On a given day, you can choose one of the problems for groups to solve, or – if you have several problems that seem to require immediate solutions – give a different problem to each group. During the feedback discussion, the recorders can announce their solutions. Students who handed in a problem will listen attentively to the solutions offered by their peers.
- Lastly, you might give them a personal problem that you have been unable to solve. I shall always remember how my writing class in 1980 solved my problem and virtually changed my teaching career. I asked them, "I do not want to take home marking any more. Got any suggestions?" They came up with so many ideas that I developed an entire "survival" system for teaching composition in which we set up a "newspaper-like" classroom, filled with writers and editors. I became the chief editor and conducted final one-to-one tutorials to ready student products for their intended audiences. As a result, by the end of the term, students had written more than ever before and improved their standard of writing dramatically, and I had freed up my evenings and weekends and started to write books. Seven books later, here I am. Such is the power of Personal Problem-Solving workshops.

Social Problem-Solving

- Handle this workshop in the same way as the Personal Problem-Solving workshop but provide social problems to solve: overpopulation of the Earth, the greenhouse effect, AIDS, the environment, drugs, alcohol, etc.

Political Problem-Solving

- Handle this workshop in the same way as the Personal Problem-Solving workshop but provide political problems to solve: Which political party will best help to improve education? Which country has the most democratic system? What features of other countries' political systems should we adopt in our country? Should Quebec become a separate country from Canada? How would you resolve the Middle East hostage issue?

Scholastic Problem-Solving

- Handle this workshop in the same way as the Personal Problem-Solving workshop but provide scholastic problems to solve: By the time we graduate, which jobs will be open to us? What should you do if you find that you are failing a course? How can I become a Master Student?

Course-Content Problem-Solving

- This workshop works the same way as the Personal Problem-Solving workshop, except that the problems are course oriented. You can choose either to give all groups the same problems and have them share their results with the class afterwards, or to give different problems to each group and have them share their problems and solutions with the class. Healthy discussions can follow each variation.
- Some problems I have used with English Lit groups included:
  - If you were a member of the Fox family (from Paul Theroux's *The Mosquito Coast*) what would you have insisted the family do after Allie blew up Fat Boy? Each member of the group should assume the role of one of the characters: Mother, Charlie, Jerry, one of the twins, or perhaps Mr. Haddy.
  - Which Emily Dickinson poem best represents her style? Each group member should select a Dickinson poem and discuss its style. Together, the group should determine Dickinson's overall style and select one poem that best illustrates her style.
  - Which of Oliver Stone's films is his best? After viewing all of Stone's films (and reading professional reviews), the group should determine which film it thinks is the best.

- For subjects across the curriculum, you might present a range of problems:
  - Which country suffered the most from the Vietnam War? (Students can each assume a different country's position.)
  - How can we best clean up an ocean oil spill?
  - How can we persuade the entire school population to become physically fit?

YOUR OWN IDEAS FOR COURSE-CONTENT PROBLEMS

Playing Detective

Teacher Preparation: Ask students to study a small portion of course content on their own, making sure that they know and understand it to the best of their abilities before you engage them in the workshop.

Length of Time: 10 to 15 minutes, depending on the length of material and complexity of the problem.

- After students have studied a portion of course content (a poem, a character sketch, a recipe, a how-to manual, etc.), pose a problem to them based on the material. Then choose five or six students who will act as leaders and talk to them privately. Say something like, "I want each of you to come up with your own solutions to this problem based on the content material." Depending on the content material, the solution may be an interpretation, a mathematical equation, a country's main industry, a missing link, a cause, a contrast, etc.

- Each leader should then form a group with five or six other students who will try to discover the leader's chosen solution by asking questions that require a "Yes" or "No" answer. As the members of each group hear the leader's answers, they should see whether they can arrive at a solution. When one student has discovered a solution, he/she should announce, "I have the solution!" The leader should invite the student to solve the problem. If the leader is not satisfied with the solution, she/he should invite the group to ask more questions.

- Here's an example of how Playing Detective works: Ask the whole class to read "Richard Cory" silently.

Richard Cory

by Edwin Arlington Robinson

Whenever Richard Cory went down town,
We people on the pavement looked at him:
He was a gentleman from sole to crown,
Clean favored, and imperially slim.

And he was always quietly arrayed,
And he was always human when he talked;
But still he fluttered pulses when he said,
"Good-morning," and he glittered when he walked.

And he was rich — yes, richer than a king —
And admirably schooled in every grace:
In fine, we thought that he was everything
To make us wish that we were in his place.

So on we worked, and waited for the light,
And went without the meat, and cursed the bread;
And Richard Cory, one calm summer night,
Went home and put a bullet through his head.

- Call upon five students (your better ones); they will act as leaders of the workshop and roleplay Richard Cory. Ask the five Richard Corys: "Why did you put a bullet through your head?"

- Members of each group will ask Richard Cory questions to determine why he committed suicide, such as:
  - Was Richard Cory your real name?
  - Were you a killer?
  - Did you have lots of money?
  - Did you run a large business?
  - Were you gay?
  - Did you have AIDS?
  - Were you really handsome?
- In a follow-up class discussion, decide which Richard Cory solution is most probable.
- Think of material that you might ask students to use in Playing Detective. Here are a few situations to help you get started:
  - After studying Plato's account of the death of Socrates: "Why did Socrates drink the hemlock?"
  - After studying the ramifications of Meech Lake: "Why did Premier Wells of Newfoundland reject the new Canadian constitutional proposal?"
  - After a group of home economics students entered a sewing contest: "Why did Jane's dress win first prize?"

YOUR OWN IDEAS FOR PLAYING DETECTIVE

Victim Theory

Teacher Preparation: Select a number of real people or fictional characters that you want your students to examine in detail.
Length of Time: 10 to 15 minutes.

- In her book, "*Survival,*" Margaret Atwood examines characters in terms of their being victimized. She talks about victims falling into four categories or "positions":
    - **Position One** victims deny that they are victims despite evidence to the contrary. Position One victims rationalize that they are better off than others and do not complain because they are afraid they may lose their privileges.
    - **Position Two** victims acknowledge that they are victims, but as a result of fate or the will of God. Position Two victims do not look at the real causes of their victimization.
    - **Position Three** victims acknowledge they are victims, but refuse to accept that they have to remain victims. Position Three victims identify their source of oppression, channel their energy into constructive action, and take action to change their position.
    - **Position Four** victims consider themselves "creative non-victims." They become creative individuals, accepting the fact that they "have to" do some things;for example, go to work. Instead of feeling like victims, however, they enjoy the experience without suppressing their feelings.
- After students understand and appreciate the four positions, arrange them in groups of four. Give each group the name of a different fictitious or real person, for example, Macbeth, Scout Finch, Churchill, Madonna, Margaret Thatcher. If the class is studying a novel, give each group a different main character; if a period of history, a different historical figure, etc.
- Each student assumes a different "victim" position (1, 2, 3, or 4) and in a discussion roleplays the character to convince the others in the group that the character occupies that position. In other words, the group conducts a "four-way split-personality" conversation, arguing about which kind of victim the group's assigned character really is.
- As a follow-up, the most convincing "victim" from each group can report to the class why he/she is in that position.
- For an interesting discussion in a psychology class, you might divide your class into groups and have each student determine, through discussion in the group, his or her own victim position.

YOUR OWN IDEAS FOR PROBLEM-SOLVING WORKSHOPS

CHAPTER FOURTEEN

Researching

Students need a good foundation of research skills for many of their courses. Getting them to appreciate the techniques of researching by completing a few personal and informal workshops before producing a formal research paper will often allay their fears about undertaking formal research.

Personal Group Research

Teacher Preparation: Set aside time before a formal research assignment for students to work on this workshop.
Length of Time: 10 minutes.

- Ask students to form groups of three with students they do not know too well. Their task, in ten minutes of discussion, is to find out how many things — besides attending the same school and enrolling in your class – they have in common. Let them go about the task as they wish, as long as they discover what they all have in common. They may find out in their discussion that they all ride a bike, have a younger sister, belong to the same religion, etc.
- After ten minutes, have a spokesperson from each group share the things they have in common. You might ask them what research skills they used to make some of their discoveries.

Shield Research Project

Teacher Preparation: If your purpose is to teach students research skills, consider having them work on something personal that will really interest them and their families instead of topics that will merely "keep them busy."
Length of Time: The same amount of time you would use if assigning a formal research paper.

- Ask students to produce a family shield, based on their research. My students always find the project interesting to work on, and their classmates and families always enjoy the results.
- You can use this workshop in connection with your school's traditions or an Open House display (See Chapter 10). Duplicate (or modify) the following instructions.

Family Shield

The project has three steps:

1. **A Personal Family Shield**
   - Design a shield to exhibit your personal symbols. You might wish to include some of your family's symbols as well.
   - Consider the shape and colors of your shield. Consult books of heraldry to see the different kinds of shields available.
   - Include four to six symbols. More might clutter your shield.
   - The shield should reveal symbolically your family background and your interests, dreams, ideals, beliefs, values, aspirations, hopes, and personality.
   - The shield should have a motto on it which will reflect your philosophy of life. It should be in Latin unless you ask for and receive special permission to use another language. To find a suitable quotation, find one in English in *Bartlett's*. Then look up the basic words in a Latin dictionary in the library and take them to someone who knows Latin to put in correct form.
   - On SHIELD DAY, _____ (date), you will be asked to give a one-minute talk on your shield to whoever asks.
   - The shields will be on display on the bulletin board for others to see.

2. **Research**
   After researching all of the parts of your shield, you should produce a minimum of _____ research cards. Each card should give the full book title and include relevant notes with a page number for all material used.

3. **Written Presentation and Bibliography**
   You must produce a 250-word paper, giving a full explanation of your shield, and a full bibliography according to the MLA guidelines.

Library Tour

Teacher Preparation: Ask a librarian to come to your class (or have your class visit the library) to arrange a library tour.
Length of time: One class period.

- Letting a librarian talk to students about the library has more benefits than giving details about the library yourself. For one thing, the students get to know the librarian and when they are there alone, they will not hesitate to ask her or him questions. Sometimes librarians will take students on a tour and give them special handouts to help them use the library efficiently. My college's librarians give a quiz to the students after the tour, which they mark and return to the students. Check to see if a library tour is available at your school.

Library Treasure Hunt

Teacher Preparation: Make up a series of questions based on course content.
Answers to the questions should be in books in the library, not the textbook.
As well, duplicate the answer form below (or make up one yourself).
Length of Time: One class period.

- On separate pieces of paper, make up enough questions based on the content of your course so that each student can receive two. You might, for example, go through the text and find allusions that require more knowledge before students really understand the reference. Beside the question, you might put the page number from the textbook so that students can see exactly where you got the idea for the question.
- Put all the questions in a hat and on a given day have students draw two questions each. It is their responsibility to find the answers (in the library) before the end of the period. Let the librarian(s) know that your class is doing the Treasure Hunt and ask them *not* to help. Students are on their own in order to see how well they can use the card catalogue, microfiche, stacks, periodical guides, etc.
- On a separate piece of paper, have students put the two questions in one column, the source or sources they used to find the answer in another column, and the answer to the question in the last column. Here is an example; modify it to suit your needs.

Questions	Sources	Answers
1.		
2.		

Small-Group Mini-Research Essay

Teacher Preparation: Adapt the material from the Collaborative Writing workshop (Chapter Four) so that small groups of students can work on a single, short research essay.
Length of Time: 3 or 4 periods, depending on the complexity of the assignment.

- Each group of students should make a list of five or six questions (social, political, or based on course content), then pass the list to another group to choose one that interests them. The first group must collectively write a research paper, answering that question.

- Besides taking on the roles of Leader, Observer, Time Keeper, and Recorder (outlined in Chapter Thirteen), students should take on responsibilities for researching and writing so that they do not duplicate work. For example, one can be responsible for researching books in print; another, magazines and newspapers; another, audio-visual material; and another can interview. Each must make sure to gather complete bibliographic details. When they have gathered all the material, one can be responsible for writing the opening and closing, two for writing the body of the mini-paper, and one for making sure that the set-up of the parenthetical citations and bibliography is accurate. That student must make sure to find out which bibliographic form you require: APA, MLA, footnotes, etc.
- After each group has completed the paper, you can conduct a one-to-four editing session (Chapter Five). The publication of the paper occurs when the groups exchange their mini-research essays. Discussion and thank-you letters can follow. Once students have worked on a mini-research essay within a small group, they should be able to write a solo research essay with greater confidence.

YOUR OWN IDEAS FOR RESEARCHING

CHAPTER FIFTEEN

Essay Writing

For years, after I taught a body of material, I would ask my students to write a long essay or report as a culminating assignment. Taking these assignments home, I would read and grade them. Returning the assignment to each individual student with an occasional comment for all to hear, I relentlessly kept the learning process between me and the student. Few students shared their assignments with other students. Where they ended up was anyone's guess.

Since introducing active learning into my classes and realizing the importance of setting up a classroom learning community, I enjoy watching the sharing that goes on among the students. In fact, I have on occasion had a few students see me privately to try to convince me to raise a mark on a fellow-student's assignment because they thought it was worth more than the mark I gave. A real sense of community learning!

The workshops in this chapter encourage cooperation among students. Students experience the joys and benefits as well as the shortcomings of cooperative learning. They learn to give and take. They learn to adapt and evaluate. They learn to sift through material, analyzing it for useful information. Finally, they learn to blend material from various sources to produce a synthesis for which they can claim ownership.

Even the most dedicated teachers of active learning will appreciate the necessity of having their students write essays and will endeavor to provide opportunities for their students to express their ideas on paper. But essay writing should not be the responsibility of teachers of English only. From time to time, teachers in all subjects should encourage their students to write essays. In doing so, they will help raise the standard of writing. Imagine the results if students in non-English classes had to write an essay each month!

You might think that you have no time to introduce writing into your classes; with so much content to get through, there's no time for essay writing. By asking students to write even an occasional paragraph, you will be sending a clear message to both students and your English-teaching colleagues that you believe writing *is* important. Math teachers of my acquaintance have turned their students' thinking around by asking their students for assignments such as, "Write a short paragraph to a student who missed yesterday's class to explain how you divide by decimals. Use a couple of illustrations in your paragraph."

Occasionally you might like to suggest to one of your English colleagues that you assign an essay topic and that, in their composition class, students go through their various writing processes: establish writing variables with you as the intended audience, and organize editing and revising sessions to ensure that the essay will receive a good mark. Once you have graded the essays, talk with your English colleague about the quality of the essays. Doubtless you will see that the essays are much better than the ones written without this kind of team teaching.

If you don't like that idea, and you are a non-English teacher, you might encourage your English department to set up a Writing Associates Programs (See Chapter 5 for details).

The active-learning workshops below deal with topic and thesis statements, and various organizational techniques that will help students write good essays. Other parts of *Workshops for Active Learning* also encourage quality writing, and in order to raise the standard of writing across the grades and across the curriculum, you are encouraged to take your students through workshops in Chapters Four and Fourteen, and any others that interest you.

Helping students compose a topic sentence for a paragraph or a thesis statement for an essay is perhaps the most important thing you can do to ensure they compose well-organized pieces of writing. Topic and thesis sentences not only point readers in the right direction, they also act as signposts for writers, ensuring that they will follow the initial directions that they are thinking about and end up where they want to go.

Although you can go to various composition textbooks to study the finer points of topic and thesis statements, you might like to plunge into the following workshop with your students right away.

Topic Sentence Creation

> *Teacher Preparation*: Think of several broad topics that you would like your students to narrow down so that they could write a single paragraph. Duplicate the diagrams below, or adapt them to fit your needs.
> *Length of Time*: One class period.

- In groups of three or four, students should study these diagrams to see how to narrow a topic from a broad one and come up with a topic sentence:

BROAD TOPIC (a large subject)
|
LIMITED TOPIC (a specific subject)
|
A MORE LIMITED TOPIC (suitable for a paragraph)
|
POINT OF VIEW (the main focus)
|
TOPIC SENTENCE

EDUCATION
|
POST-SECONDARY EDUCATION
|
COLLEGE
|
THE BENEFITS OF GOING TO COLLEGE
|
(POSSIBLE TOPIC SENTENCES)

A college provides a better education than a vocational school.

Not everyone benefits from going to college.

A college is a good place to meet people.

• Give students several broad topics dealing with aspects of your course. Together, members of each group should narrow the topics and compose several possible topic sentences suitable for a one-paragraph response. When they have finished, have them evaluate their topic sentences and choose one. They should also decide how they would develop the paragraph (chronologically, spatially, climactically, sequentially, or by using comparison/contrast, cause/effect, classification/division, restatements, definition, general to particular, etc.). Leaders from each group should put their topic sentences on the board or overhead transparency and indicate what the paragraph will contain. Other students and you can evaluate the topic sentences, determining which ones will lead both writers and readers to a logical destination.

Thesis Statement Creation

Teacher Preparation: Think of several broad topics that you would like your students to narrow down so that they could write a full essay. Duplicate the diagrams below, or adapt them to fit your needs.
Length of Time: One class period.

• In groups of three or four, students should study these diagrams to see how to narrow a topic from a broad one and come up with a thesis statement – with appropriate topic sentences:

BROAD TOPIC (a large subject)
|
LIMITED TOPIC (a specific subject)
|
A MORE LIMITED TOPIC (suitable for an essay)
|
POINT OF VIEW (the main focus)
|
THESIS STATEMENT (a sentence that controls the main idea)
| | |
TOPIC SENTENCE TOPIC SENTENCE TOPIC SENTENCE
(A sentence that controls the main idea for each paragraph)

ARACHNIDS
|
SPIDERS
|
SPIDERS IN THE U.S.
|
POISONOUS SPIDERS IN THE U.S.
|
Two spiders found in the U.S. produce poisons that can cause severe local or general reactions in their victims.
| |
The black widow is notorious for both its distinctive appearance and its poisonous bite. | The brown recluse, though not as well known as the black widow and very different in appearance, has a bite that causes severe reactions.

- Give students several large topics dealing with aspects of your course. Together, members of each group should narrow each topic and compose an appropriate thesis statement and a suitable number of topic sentences that will develop the thesis fully. They should also decide how they would develop each paragraph. When they have finished, have the leaders put their thesis statements and topic sentences on the board or overhead transparencies and indicate what the whole essay (and each paragraph) will contain. Other students and you can evaluate each thesis statement and its topic sentences, determining which ones will lead both writers and readers to a logical destination.

Limiting and Focusing a Topic

Teacher Preparation: Think of topics (or allow students to think of their own) on which you would like your students to focus. Duplicate or adapt the diagrams below.

Length of Time: One class period.

- Helping students to come up with a suitable focus and ultimately a successful piece of writing depends on your giving them opportunities to choose topics that interest them. They then need to be able to limit their topic to a manageable size and consider their narrow topic in terms of the writing variables: audience, purpose, format, voice, and point of view. Using each writing variable to flesh out their limited topics, students will arrive at the precise focus they want. This workshop will help them limit, focus, and come up with interesting and workable thesis statements or topic sentences.
- Have students choose partners. Together, they should choose a broad topic. Independently, they should each complete the following chart and, when both have finished, compare and discuss their choices. Then each should talk about the best ways to develop the piece of writing.

Broad Topic: _____

Audience: _____

Purpose: _____

Format: _____

Voice: _____

Point of View: _____

Limited Topic: _____

Thesis Statement: _____

_____

First Topic Sentence: _____

_____

Second Topic Sentence: _____

_____

Third Topic Sentence: _____

_____

- If students are writing a one-paragraph response, replace "thesis statement" with "topic sentence" and omit the first, second, third topic sentences before you duplicate the chart.
- Repeat this workshop several times so that students have lots of practice and plenty of opportunities to ask questions. Instead of working in pairs, students can work in small groups.

Organizing with Cards

Teacher and Student Preparation: After you complete a unit of course content, ask students to bring a set of 3x5 index cards (or similar size pieces of paper).

Length of Time: One class period.

* This workshop is designed to take students from not knowing what to write about to having a well-focused, limited topic with corresponding thesis and topic sentences and with methods of organization established.
* Before starting this workshop, students should be familiar with the preceding workshop, "Limiting and Focusing a Topic."
* Adapt these instructions (written for students) to fit your needs. Feel free to move about during the workshop so that you can assist when needed.
  - For two to five minutes, write, on separate cards, different ideas (based on the material you've recently learned) to use as possible essay topics. Try for ten different topics!
  - For a minute, look through your cards and choose three that you would like to consider. Put the others aside. Then, remove two cards so that you are left with the topic that interests you most.
  - If your topic isn't narrow enough, try limiting it to a workable one.
  - For ten minutes, write different things about your limited topic, each on a separate card. You can write single words, phrases, sentences, quotations, causes, effects, comparisons, contrasts, examples, details, illustrations – anything that you might use to develop your essay. Write as quickly as possible so that you use 30 or 40 cards.
* After the students have brainstormed for about ten minutes, break in with a few probing questions or suggestions so that they can fill out many more cards – especially if they are writing a long essay. Make up questions that you think will lead your students to write useful information on each card. After asking the question, give them time to write one response on each card. Here are some I ask:
  - What do you like most about your topic?
  - What do you like least?
  - If you had to teach your topic to a class, what four things would you make sure to include? Write one per card.
  - What would you like to tell your mother about your topic?
  - Classify your topic.
  - Divide your topic.
  - Using two cards, write down all the good and bad things about your topic.
  - Is your topic a cause or an effect? What came before? What comes after?
  - Define your topic.
  - How is your topic like a leaking faucet?
  - Write a simile – "My topic is like a ...."
  - What symbol comes to mind when you think of your topic?
  - What do you think that you need to research about your topic? Write different things on separate cards. Where do you think you will find the necessary information?
  - When your reader first sees your topic, what question will he/she probably ask?
  - How will you answer the question?

- After ten minutes of questioning, they will have a large pile of cards. To help them organize the cards, give them the following instructions:
    - For five minutes sort the cards into common piles: good things about your topic, bad things, causes, effects, reasons, results, examples, a process, excuses, etc. As you organize the cards into different piles, you may want to make up additional cards. Do so, and add them to the appropriate piles.
    - When you have several piles, see if your can merge two piles because of a similarity between them. Put piles of one or two cards, that you cannot merge, aside. Limit the number of piles to no more than four. Place a blank card on top of each pile and write on it what each pile of cards has in common.
    - For five minutes, sitting on the floor, place the card with your essay topic on it in front of you. Then arrange each of the cards from the first pile in a logical order (chronologically, climactically, sequentially, spatially, etc.) under the Main Topic card. Then arrange the cards from the other piles in a logical order. If some cards don't fit logically anywhere in your organization, put them aside. As you are arranging your cards, you will probably think of additional details. Put the information on separate cards and place them in the correct positions. When you have finished arranging the piles, decide whether your first pile should be moved into the second, third, or fourth position. In other words, think about what you will develop first in your essay, second, third, and so forth. Have a valid reason for your order of development.
    - Call one of your classmates over to look at your cards. For five minutes, share the topic of your essay with your classmate and brainstorm with him or her. Explain your point of view and all of your writing variables. Also explain how you intend to organize your essay. Ask for feedback.
    - When you are satisfied with your organization, make an outline from your cards and begin to draft your essay. Good luck.

Twenty-Minute Workshops

Teacher Preparation: None required.
Length of Time: 20 minutes.

- If you want to test your students' knowledge of course material, and in addition introduce a stylistic or mechanical feature that they can add to their writing, have them do what I call a *Twenty-Minute Workshop*. Many of the ideas behind these workshops are quite simple: for example, you can ask students to write a 100-word summary of a chapter in which each sentence must contain a semicolon, or a verbal phrase, or the summary must contain six transitional devices or all periodic sentences. By engaging in a different Twenty-Minute Workshop each day, students master the fundamentals of writing by focusing on their own writing instead of artificial handbooks and meaningless worksheets. They are in charge of their own mechanics. As well, they are reviewing course content.
- I have found Twenty-Minute Workshops so useful that I have composed nearly a hundred of them (some simple, some sophisticated). You might want to make up some of your own, or if you'd like to order a copy of my book, *The Twenty-Minute Workshop*, contact me.
- The following is a sample workshop that is easy to complete and easier to edit.

MONOSYLLABLE POWER

IF YOU ARE OVER-USING ABSTRACT WORDS, try monosyllables.

Writer's Warm-up

Are you aware that many of our most important words are monosyllables? Here are a few: love, live, birth, work, sex, sleep, health, eat, rich, poor, sun, good, God, hope, fun, food.

Practice Time

Individually or collaboratively, make a list of ten different monosyllabic words. When you have finished, compare your list with those of other students. Check to make sure that each word is monosyllabic.

Back and Forth Game

In pairs or small groups, one person gives another a monosyllabic word. The other person must come up with a monosyllabic word that begins with the last letter of the previous word, for example, *man, now, war, r....* The game ends when a player cannot think of a word that no one has used thus far in the game.
Object of the Game: present a word that ends with a letter that will stump your opponent.

Writer's Workout

Using only monosyllables in a piece of writing, you are forced to concentrate on the importance of every word you choose. Read what Roger Garrison was able to produce by using monosyllables.

from *How a Writer Works*

We are too rich in words, and hence we tend to waste them. Long words tempt us, since they seem to show that we know more than we do. But short words do not let us hide what we do not know. These are words we use each day to tell us how we feel or what we think. When we love, we want to hug or kiss or say soft things. If we feel joy, we may sing or dance. If we feel hate, our words are harsh and we may curse. Short words tell what we are: they are strong and say what is real.

Writer's Demonstration

Now write your piece on a topic that interests you. Instead of a paragraph, you might like to write a poem or an advertisement. Brainstorm for support so that you can develop your topic fully. Make sure, however, that you use only words of one syllable.

Editors' Evaluation

Check to see that all words are of one syllable. For any that are not, think of new words with one syllable that will fit the content, style, and sense of the entire piece.

Hint: By incorporating twenty-minute workshops into non-English classrooms, you will certainly improve the standard of writing among your students, at the same time ensuring that they know the course material.

IDEAS FOR ESSAY-WRITING WORKSHOPS

IDEAS FOR ESSAY-WRITING WORKSHOPS

CHAPTER SIXTEEN

Films

On many occasions, you might wish to show films to your students. Sometimes, instead of showing them yourself, you might like to ask for a volunteer to show the film while you teach him/her how to lower the screen, thread the machine, take care of volume, etc. For the next film, the volunteer teaches the same things to another student. Then, that volunteer teaches another, and so on and so on until a large number of students know how to show films, instead of overworking one student and thus having only one expert in the room.

Instead of introducing the films and conducting follow-up discussions yourself, involve students in Pre-viewing and Post-viewing workshops so that they become actively involved in helping other students view the films. Before they start to work on their Pre- and Post-viewing workshops, you might like to conduct a Desktop Teaching workshop (Chapter Seven) on film terminology. Then, duplicate or adapt the following suggestions to fit your needs.

Hints on Film Viewing

To help you appreciate the films fully, you will join a panel of students. Sign up under the title of one of the films we will be seeing this term. No more than six can sign up for one film.

Dividing the workload any way you wish, prepare to conduct pre-viewing and post-viewing workshops on your chosen film.
You may choose to have all members present at both workshops or divide the group so that one part handles the pre-viewing while the other handles the post-viewing.

It might be a good idea to appoint a leader who will organize the group and assign duties; however, the project should remain democratic.

Hints for both workshops:
Try to have a unifying theme for your presentations, so that they are more than students taking turns talking. Do not read your notes. Use your imagination; the more synthesizing you do, the better. You should have someone in charge of each workshop in order to encourage audience participation and questions.

The more you involve the rest of the class in the workshops, the better! Your goal is not to make a brilliant presentation in which the other students sit passively and listen to you.

Pre-viewing a Film

Teacher Preparation: Duplicate or adapt the following information for the students' use.

Length of Time: Depending on the length of the film, the Pre-viewing workshop should range from 10 to 30 minutes.

Pre-viewing a Film

Your main task is to help your audience view the film. Let them know what to expect, without telling too much of the plot. You might, if you wish, get hold of the film and watch it in order to help you with the workshop. You might share interesting details about the director, producer, camera operator, designers, and actors or refer to other films they have done. If the film is based on a play or novel, tell your audience a few details about the task of bringing it to the screen. Who, for example, adapted it for the screen? What differences between the novel and film should viewers look for? Consult reviews to let them know what others think about the film. If the film is a documentary, link the course material to the film. Finally, share any detail that you think would help your listeners appreciate the film more.

Above all, though, incorporate the above suggestions in active-learning workshops instead of standing in front of the class and merely reading all the facts.

Post-viewing a Film

Teacher Preparation: Duplicate or adapt the following information for your students' use.

Length of Time: 10 to 30 minutes, depending on the length of the film.

Post-viewing a Film

Each presenter should choose a different aspect of the film to analyze, for example, movement, editing, literary value, photography, acting, directing, *mise en scène*, etc. It might be a good idea for the group to get together for a runthrough before presenting the post-viewing workshop to ensure that you cover all the important points of the film.

Try to relate the pre-viewing and post-viewing workshops; if, for example, members of the pre-viewing workshop suggested that viewers watch for significant aspects of the film, you might want to conduct a session to hear your audience's reaction.

Above all, though, devise active-learning activities so that your audience are not just sitting, listening to you.

• I give my students a written evaluation and a group mark, which they divide among themselves. Change any portion of this evaluation sheet to fit your needs.

Grades and comments for Pre- and Post-viewing Workshops.

Film _____ Section _____

Comments for Group Work on Pre-viewing Workshop:

Comments for Group Work on Post-viewing workshop:

Overall Grade for the workshop: ____ (out of 5). Take this mark and multiply it by the number of people in your group ( ). This will give you a total of _____. Conduct a short meeting and share the mark within your group. Make sure that each member *signs* his/her own name and records the mark in the spaces below. If you all contributed equally to the presentation, you should receive the same mark; if, on the other hand, one of you did far less than the others and one far more than the others, you may decide to distribute the marks accordingly. At any rate, you should have a fine time negotiating. (If you run into difficulties, call on me.) Hand this grading sheet back to me as soon as possible so that I can record the marks.

List names of members of your group and their marks:

_____ ____   _____ ____

_____ ____   _____ ____

_____ ____   _____ ____

IDEAS FOR FILM WORKSHOPS

Higher-Level Thinking Skills

Many educators consider that students do not really begin to learn until they know and comprehend the material to be learned. In fact, they give little or no credit to students who can recite material by rote or even demonstrate an understanding of what they have learned. If your own education was anything like mine, you will recall sitting through dozens of exams trying to supply exact words to "Fill in the Blanks" or the exact circumstances of a quotation from a play so that you could answer questions like: "Who said this? To Whom? Under what circumstances?" (sometimes even "In which Act and Scene?"), and finally, "What is the significance of the quotation?"

I will never forget a major portion of my final exam for a Master's course on Musical Comedy Direction: "Here are 100 song titles. Name the musical each came from." All term we were warned by other students that we had to know all the song titles from all the musicals ever written. So, when "September Song" appeared, I was able to write *Knickerbocker Holiday* in the blank. Ugh! (I learned them, by the way, in my own way. I wrote a love letter to my fiancée in which I blended 200 or so song titles. I told her that the next time we met I'd give her a kiss for every title she could identify and something even more special if she could name the musical the song came from. We had a glorious and exhausting weekend when she came for a visit to my campus digs.)

After completing the workshop "Connecting the Thinking Process and Course Content" (Chapter 2) a few times and after seeing the value of cultivating their higher-level cognitive thinking skills, your students will be ready for the six chapters in this section. While working through these chapters, however, you might like to blend one workshop with another so that you get double duty out of the time available.

IDEAS FOR BLENDING TWO OR MORE WORKSHOPS

In the next six chapters, I suggest that you encourage students to compose questions that will help them develop high-level thinking skills. Let them practice making up several questions, using the key words in each chapter. They can answer their own questions; they can share them with a partner and answer each other's; they can post them for the whole class to answer.

QUICK REFERENCE TO MOST SUCCESSFUL WORKSHOPS IN SECTION THREE

WORKSHOPS	PAGE

CHAPTER SEVENTEEN

Knowledge

It may be true that a little knowledge is a dangerous thing, but if students have not experienced the material to be learned and do not know it, the learning process comes to an abrupt halt. Knowing the facts, therefore, is the first important step in learning and in developing thinking skills. Students must, however, realize that knowing facts and details about the course content is just the beginning of their learning process. In fact, memorizing lists of facts trivializes the learning process.

During their early grades, students are inundated with facts, and it seems right and just that teachers help students remember information in order to add to their storehouse of knowledge. In later grades, however, students easily become surfeited with information, feeling that their brains cannot possibly hold one more fact. If memorizing facts and details continues to be considered the most important part of the learning process, students can easily turn off and live for the day that they can quit school. Teachers must work to make students independent learners by de-emphasizing rote knowledge and training them to use resource books such as dictionaries, textbooks, and their journals (filled with important facts that they don't want to store in their memories) to help them move to a higher stage of the learning process. We must prevent students from feeling like George from Lorraine Hansberry's *A Raisin in the Sun*, as he describes his educational experience:

It's simple. You read books – to learn facts – to get grades – to pass the course – to get a degree. That's all – it has nothing to do with thoughts.

Key Words to Stimulate Knowledge

Teacher Preparation: Prepare a sample three-part knowledge question based on some aspect of course content for demonstration purposes. Make an overhead transparency of the knowledge key words, boxed in Chapter 2.
Length of Time: 15 minutes.

- Help students to make up three-part knowledge questions along the lines outlined in Chapter Six. Suggest that they choose words from the following list: **define, state, list, label, reproduce, paraphrase, explain in your own words, summarize, give the exact denotative meaning**.
- As a class, make up a few Knowledge questions, making sure that each contains a key word, an object, and a limiting factor. After students make up a few, carry on a class evaluation discussion. You might interject a few questions like "What's the key word in that question? Do you really understand the object of this question? Is there a limiting factor in that question?"

• Duplicate the following example or make up one of your own:

Three-part Knowledge Question

"List the three isotopes of carbon."

Key Word: list
Object: to state in which forms the element carbon naturally
                        occurs
Limiting Factor: include forms of elemental carbon only

Distribute your Lecture Notes

> *Teacher Preparation*: Duplicate your lecture notes on a unit of course content. Compose some open-ended statements and questions on the content to test your students' knowledge of the content along the lines of the Student Knowledge workshop below.
>
> *Length of Time*: 10 minutes for the open-ended statements and questions; 5 minutes for a follow-up discussion to clarify any "lost" knowledge; the rest of the period to involve students in application workshops.

• After many years of hesitation, I finally duplicated a set of my lecture notes and gave it to a class the day before I planned to give the lecture. When the class met the next day, both they and I "knew" the material. After engaging students in a brief, small-group Motivation workshop (Chapter Two) to test their knowledge of the material, I was able to spend the rest of the period in worthwhile workshops so that students applied the material to both real-life and imaginary situations. Instead of my asking questions all period, students asked questions, solved problems, roleplayed, and generally displayed their knowledge of the material through higher-level thinking activities. Without doubt, the lesson was one of the most successful I experienced.

• So, when you wish to involve your class in active-learning workshops, distribute your lecture notes so that you and your class can meet on relatively equal terms, both "knowing" the material to be learned. Naturally, you will know more about the material than they; however, make sure not to deal too early with facts and details that perhaps need further, deeper knowledge of the subject. Leave additional material to another lesson, another set of lecture notes. Instead, involve your students in some of the following workshops. Later, when students really know the material, you will be able to involve them in comprehension, analysis, application, and evaluation of the information from your lecture notes. (See workshops in the following chapters.)

Student Knowledge

Teacher Preparation: Provide a series of open-ended statements and questions based on a unit of material you intend to teach.

Length of Time: 10 minutes for student responses; 5 minutes for class discussion.

- Students enter your classroom with varying degrees of knowledge of the material you are going to teach, from everything on the topic to just a smattering of the material.
- Administering a small-group workshop to determine what students already know about the material can help you determine how to teach a lesson. After students have arranged themselves in small groups, give them a handout of questions or open-ended statements based on the essential content of the material. Together, students respond to the questions or complete the statements; those who know the answers will help those who do not.
- In a follow-up discussion, leaders from each group can report their responses to the items on the handout. If one group does not know the answers to some of the questions or cannot complete some of the open-ended statements, ask other groups to provide responses. The student discussions can become highly interactive. (Occasionally, you can ask a group if they are satisfied with a response. If they are not, the group must probe more deeply and provide a better response.) If a large number of questions or statements remain unanswered, you will know what you need to teach; if, on the other hand, students have responded to nearly all of the items on the handout, you can move confidently to the next portion of the course content.
- This workshop will help you determine not only your students' knowledge of part of the course content but also your approach to teaching the material. Nothing is more unfruitful than trying to teaching students something that they already know. When I hear a first-year college English instructor say to a class – in all sincerity and earnestness – "A noun is the name of a person, place, or thing," I despair. Many of those hapless students have been told the same thing about nouns since third grade.
- All teachers must begin to place responsibility for knowing the basics of their course content firmly on the shoulders of students, and not waste valuable class time testing students' knowledge with meaningless worksheets and quizzes. Rather, students should be constantly using basic knowledge by writing, talking, analyzing, applying, evaluating, and/or synthesizing *every day*.
- The following workshops are recommended for students who need knowledge of the facts to develop their higher-level cognitive thinking skills.

Knowledge Drills

Teacher Preparation: For a difficult portion of course content, especially one filled with facts and details you consider important for your students to remember, engage them in drills.

Length of Time: Keep the workshops short, but repeat them a few times to ensure that students know the material.

* No doubt, you have developed during your teaching career a series of drills that work well and that you have administered to your whole class. They may take the form of flash cards to teach vocabulary or pronunciation or a diagram to show a particular procedure.
* Instead of administering these drills yourself to test students' knowledge, divide the class into groups of six to eight. Assign a body of material to each group with the instruction that each is to invent a drill to make sure that members of the group will remember the facts and details contained in the material. Students who are already familiar with many of your drills will perhaps copy yours; others (perhaps with the assistance of parents) will invent new drills. At any rate, encourage students to come up with Spelling Bees, Vocabulary Bees, Beat-the-Clock, Charts, Diagrams, Maps, Grids, Flashcards, Questions in a Hat, Crossword Puzzles, Circle Learning (Chapter 7), etc.

Knowledge Games

Teacher Preparation: Just make a few suggestions and watch the games appear.

Length of Time: In most cases the games will be played as part of a longer presentation to ensure that students know the facts.

* Instead of describing games to learn the facts, suggest that students, during group presentations, not just stand in front of the class and present facts. Instead, they should devise a game to ensure that students will remember the important details of their presentation.
* As a follow-up to a film that one group of my students showed, they played the following game with their audience: They gave each group a sheet of paper with ten questions. They also gave them twenty cards with answers (ten correct; ten incorrect). Finally, they gave each group a piece of styrofoam to which the group had to pin the ten correct answers. The group who gave the presenters the ten correct answers first won.
* Another group composed a hidden-word puzzle in which were concealed the answers to their ten questions. The students not only had to know the answers, but they had to locate them within the maze of letters and circle them. Students had to search horizontally, vertically, and diagonally, as well as backwards, for the answers. The first group to circle all ten answers won.
* Students will devise games that would never occur to you.

Twenty-Five-Word Knowledge Summary

Teacher Preparation: None required.
Length of Time: 5 to 10 minutes for evaluation of the summaries.

- Being able to summarize a portion of course content enables students to demonstrate their knowledge of the material. After they have read a chapter or other unit of material, seen a film, heard a mini-lecture, listened to a debate, etc., ask them to write a 25-word summary as a homework assignment, stating exactly what the chapter contains, what happens in the film, or what took place during the debate.
- Students should use titles of the content and authors of the material, but do *not* count them as part of the 25 words. Students should strive for exactly 25 words (not counting title and author's name) in a single sentence, although, depending on the quality and grade of your students, you may be satisfied if they write 25 words in two or three sentences.
- The Twenty-five-word Knowledge Summary not only tests students' knowledge, but also makes them aware of word choice. If they use too many words, they must cut out non-essential words; if they use too few, they must introduce essential details.
- When students come in with their 25-word summaries, ask them to post them some place in the room for all to see and evaluate, or instruct them as follows (or adapt to fit your needs).

  > Get into groups of three. Evaluate each others' 25-word summaries. Choose one that you would like to present to the rest of the class. Edit it to make sure that it contains exactly 25 words (not counting title and author's name).

- When the groups are ready, you can either have them read their summaries to the class or put them on the chalkboard. The latter method allows students, during discussion, to evaluate and rank them. Praise those students who managed to create a single, well-worded 25-word sentence that summarized the content perfectly.
- Repeat this workshop often during the term.

Building Knowledge Monthly

Teacher Preparation: Prepare a blank calendar for an upcoming month. If you have access to a computer program that prints out a blank calendar, use it. Give the calendar a title, showing the knowledge you wish students to learn each day. As well, fill in a term for the first day of the month. See below for details.
Length of Time: 5 minutes a day; 15 minutes at the end of the month for an evaluation session.

- Establish what you want your students to build during the next month: vocabulary, knowledge of terms, mythological characters, mathematical terminology, scientific symbols, or any other list of details or facts you want them to know. Give a blank calendar, like the partial one below, to each student. Each student is to complete one of the calendars for another student (as a gift), filling in a word, term, character's name, etc. in each blank space. On the first of the month, everyone exchanges calendars and for the rest of the month, everyone masters his/her own details on the calendar. At the end of the month, the students who made up the calendar test the recipients' knowledge of the contents by making up a quiz and administering it.

• Sample excerpt of a calendar:

JANUARY 1991				CHEMICAL SYMBOLS	
Monday	Tuesday	Wednesday	Thursday	Friday	Saturday
	1 NaCl	2	3	4	5

Food with Thought

Teacher Preparation: Provide a list of terms on separate pieces of paper so that students can select one. Also provide a handout that contains all of the terms so that on the day of the Food with Thought workshop, students can stroke off the terms they already know and learn those terms they do not know.

Classroom Preparation: On the day of the workshop, move desks to the edges of the room so that students can move freely.

Length of Time: 30 minutes.

• Because we often associate mealtimes with good conversation, from time to time you might like to invite students to bring a small meal to class. While eating, they can also share their thoughts on a number of topics. Adapt the following workshop to fit your grade and subject.

• Have students select a term on which to become an expert.

Breakfast with Terms (For a morning class)

• At home, students should learn as much as possible about the term they have selected, and, on a designated day, they must be prepared to be the authority on that term. They may want to wear something appropriate or bring necessary props to help illustrate their term, and if they can connect the food they have brought with the term, so much the better. All must, in some way, identify themselves by wearing the name of their term.

• If you think it necessary, you might give the students a handout of all the terms with, or without, definitions.

• Everyone's task is to have a conversation with all of the terms they do not know so that by the end of their breakfast they have become familiar with all the terms.

• The results of this workshop are quite remarkable. Students become much more relaxed, stretch their creative powers, learn helplessly. Naturally, some students excel. During a recent Breakfast with *Poetic* Terms, a student in my English Lit class became *hyperbole*. She made herself a screamingly colorful T-shirt with HYPERBOLE splashed over the front. She proceeded to pluck a grape off a cluster with, "Without doubt, this is the best grape I have ever eaten." And later after another grape, "No, I lie. *This* is the best grape I have ever eaten." Nor will the students forget what a simile is. Simile came wearing a sandwich-board with felt pens dangling on strings. He encouraged students to autograph his sandwich-board with their name within a simile.

- At the end of the class, encourage students to write in their journals what they remember about the terms. As a guide, they may use the handout. If they've forgotten any, they'll know what they have to research on their own and who to go to for help.
- Variations of this workshop that I have used: Coffee Break with Film Terms, Brunch with Literary Devices, Afternoon Tea with the Parts of Speech, Picnic with Mythic Characters, and, with my night classes, Bedtime Snack with Composition Terms.
- Another variation that has worked well near the end of term is Breakfast with the Characters. Each student chooses to come as one of the characters from the literature we studied during the term. Instead of wearing the name of the character or any overt clues, the students each wear a different number. They do not tell anyone who they are. The object of the exercise is for students to identify each character by asking them questions that *cannot* be answered by "yes" or "no." Also, students are not allowed to ask questions using the title of the selection of literature. They must rely solely on a character's actions, idiosyncracies, morals, etc.

Hint: If your list of terms is much shorter than your class enrollment, double or triple up: for example, if you wish your students to know and understand the eight parts of speech, there might be four different students teaching each one. If a student does not fully understand the term as taught by one student, all he/she has to do is seek out one of the other students who is dealing with the same term.

IDEAS FOR FOOD WITH THOUGHT

Rap Your Knowledge

Teacher Preparation: Assign a section of material that you want students to know. Divide class into pairs or small groups.

Length of Time: Give each pair or group 2 minutes to present their "rap."

- If you are wanting students to know a number of details or facts (the multiplication tables, the periodic table of chemical elements, scientific symbols, a series of dates, etc.), assign the same topic to all students, who — within pairs or small groups — will compose a "rap" song based on the material.
- On Rap Day, all students will listen intently to see how another group has "rapped their knowledge" and because they have done the same workshop, they will be in a strong position not only to appreciate what they have heard but also to evaluate it with expertise.

The Knowledge Envelope, Please

Teacher Preparation: Ask small groups of students to prepare 20 knowledge questions (using the key words above)and place them in an envelope. They can do this in class time or on their own. They should identify their envelope by giving it a name.

Length of Time: 5 minutes per envelope.

- At the beginning of the workshop, each group should sit in a circle. Each passes its envelope of questions to the group on the right. Give the groups exactly five minutes to answer all of the 20 questions, writing them on a separate piece of paper. They should write both their own group's name and the name of the envelope at the top of their answers. When the five minutes are up, they must put the questions back into the envelope and pass it to the next group to their right. They keep their answers till the end of the workshop.
- When all groups have seen all envelopes and answered all questions, ask the groups to give their answer sheets to the composers of the questions who should then mark them to find out which group *knows* the material best.
- As a follow-up, ask each group to make the announcement of the winners and to point out common errors.

YOUR OWN IDEAS FOR KNOWLEDGE WORKSHOPS

CHAPTER EIGHTEEN

Comprehension

Students quickly realize that knowing the facts and details of a course means nothing if they do not understand the significance and purpose of their newfound knowledge. Although, in reality, most people know and understand at the same time, others miss hidden meanings, significances, and overall themes because of their ignorance of or inexperience in the subject. They think to themselves, "I don't get it!" but they will forge ahead, compounding their lack of comprehension until they are hopelessly lost. It is therefore important to give students plenty of opportunities to ask questions and receive answers before they proceed to more complex, yet more rewarding, higher-level thinking strategies.

No matter how many times you might say, "Feel free to interrupt and ask questions," or "Remember, the stupid question is the one you do not ask," unsure students will be reticent to ask a question in front of their peers. Often, they may be so confused that they don't even know what questions to ask; so, during class discussions, they rely on those talkers in the room to ask questions so that they can take notes of your responses. And they often misunderstand your response because they haven't understood the relevance of the question.

Small-group workshops are the best solution to this conundrum. Depending on the sophistication of your class, you can provide them with discussion topics that will lead to their understanding of the course material. After the group discussions (with your dropping in to each group occasionally), have a spokesperson report on the group's understanding of the material. Assuming that the group has come to a consensus, you can help them refine their thinking skills by offering suggestions. Also, other groups should feel free to offer their comments, helping everyone develop a better understanding of the course material. Groups become possessive of their conclusions; they will passionately debate the merits of their point of view with other groups.

The following workshops will lead to your students' comprehension of your course content. Groups of three or four work best, so that all students have plenty of chances to talk. In the following workshops, the term "passage of material" refers to chapters from a textbook, parts of novels, episodes from TV documentaries, scenes from films, poems, etc.

Key Works to Stimulate Comprehension

Teacher Preparation: Prepare a three-part comprehension question based on a passage of material for demonstration purposes. Make an overhead transparency of the Comprehension Key Words, boxed in Chapter 2.
Length of Time: 20 minutes.

• To help students question for clear understanding of material to be comprehended, suggest that they use one of the following key words to make up a three-part question following the suggestions in Chapter 6: **separate the main point from the minor points, write a precis, summarize, illustrate,** interpret, explain, read between the lines, find the main idea, write down the main claim, state the thesis of, state the theme of, give the connotative meaning of and in no more than six word, write a complete interpretation of.

- As a follow-up, evaluate their questions in a class discussion. Help the evaluation by asking questions like, "What is (are) the key word(s) in this question? What do you think the object of that question is? If you were to answer this question, what limiting factor should you attend to?"
- Duplicate the following example or make up your own:

Three-part Comprehension Question

"Summarize the main features of the Freedom of Information Act."

Key Word:	summarize
Object:	to describe briefly what kinds of access to government documents the Freedom of Information Act allows.
Limiting Factors:	do not list all of the features of the Act, just those you think are the most important.

Student Comprehension

Teacher Preparation: None needed.
Length of Time: 10 minutes.

- If the passage of material has special significance or contains implications that you want students to recognize and appreciate, divide the class into small groups and ask each group to look for specific examples, as well as overall examples that contain a special significance to the author and readers. To find the significance or implication of a passage of material, students must be able to read between the lines, looking carefully at the *subtext*. Of course, they must already have knowledge of the text before they can comprehend the subtext.
- If students are not ready to find the significance or implications of a body of material, you might have to give them a series of questions to help them understand the text. If students have already completed several "Knowledge" workshops from the previous chapter, they probably have already touched on significance and implications in material.
- If they are ready, ask each student group to write a collective, complete sentence of no more than six words to demonstrate their understanding of the passage of material. They must arrive at a consensus of what the main idea, theme, interpretation, or thesis is before they either show it to you or announce it to the rest of the class. Moving about the room from group to group will allow you to make suggestions, point out a wasted word or two in their six-word sentence, aim their thinking in a more productive direction, and ultimately lead them to a viable interpretation of the passage of material.
- After a spokesperson reports to the rest of the class, instead of saying, "That's the correct interpretation" or "No, that's not what it means," ask other groups for their comments. If another group can point out an error in thinking, a debate between the two groups will follow; as a result (with occasional probing by you) students will arrive in the short term at a few workable interpretations and in the long term they will discover ways to read more closely. Of course, if all students are off base and cannot support their interpretation with textual evidence, they'll be interested in hearing your interpretation. Then ask them to provide textual evidence for your interpretation.

• As a variation, suggest that each group make up a question about a passage of material, using one of the Comprehension Key Words. Then they should pass their question to the group to their right. Now, each group will be working on a different comprehension question. As a follow-up, each spokesperson will read the question and the answer. The results will produce a richer appreciation of the passage of material.

A Living Short Story

Teacher Preparation: Before the workshop, take a piece of card stock (half of a large file folder will do). Cut it so that it measures about 8 1/2" x 12". With black felt pen, draw several straight lines and approximately same-sized circles so that the card looks something like this:

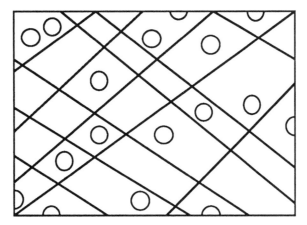

On the back, draw in light pencil your cutting lines so that you make eight separate pieces of a jigsaw puzzle – like this:

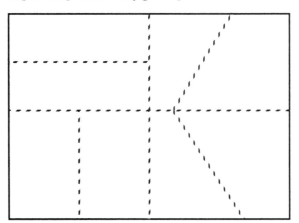

Try to make sure that several of the same-sized circles will be cut exactly in half. If there is a possibility that this will not happen, add more circles. Cut the card into eight pieces.

Classroom Preparation: In the center of the classroom, set up a small table and four chairs (or four desks all facing into each other).

Length of Time: Anywhere from 3 to 20 minutes.

• If students cannot tell the difference between reading the text and reading the subtext, do this workshop with your whole class. Ask for four volunteers. (There'll be some fun, since students won't know what they're volunteering for.) Ask each to take a place around the table. Set before each student, face down, two pieces of the puzzle.

- Number off the other students by **One**s and **Two**s. Tell them that they will need to observe and write down their observations (often while moving). They should fold a sheet of paper several times so that they can write on it while they move around.

- Tell the **One**s that they are going to observe while the four volunteers put a jigsaw puzzle together and that they are to record what each does (record only their actions – do not interpret what they are thinking). Tell the **Two**s that they are also going to observe the puzzle-makers, but they are to record only what they think is going on in their heads (record only thoughts and feelings – interpret what they are thinking). Before the volunteers start to put the puzzle together, make sure that all the **One**s and **Two**s know the volunteers' names. Then give the following instructions to the volunteers:

> There can be no talking while you put the puzzle together. You are not allowed to take a piece of the puzzle from anyone else, but you are allowed to give a piece away if you think that it fits one of the pieces you do not have. You must hand the piece *to* one of the other puzzle-makers, not place it on the desk or try to fit it onto the other piece yourself. If you have two or more pieces to give away, you must do so one at a time. If you suddenly find that you have all the pieces and cannot put the puzzle together, you may give the pieces away, either to one person or all three. The workshop ends when one person has all the pieces and puts the puzzle together himself or herself. Any questions?

- Once students know what they are doing, time them. Interrupt throughout the puzzle-making to give the time left, in order to add to the tension. (Although students usually put the puzzle together in 4 or 5 minutes, I have had a group take 18 minutes. The tension was electric. Because so many of the circles and lines might possibly connect, they did not have a sense of a simple rectangular puzzle; instead, they were trying to create a peculiarly shaped jigsaw.)

- Once the students have completed the puzzle, ask the **One**s to report on the actions (text) of the puzzle-makers. They will say things like: "Julie gave her pieces to Dick within the first 30 seconds," "Bill put five pieces together and waited for Serri to pass him the three pieces he needed." If any **One** gives interpretive responses, point out that **One**s deal with knowledge, not comprehension. Then ask the **Two**s to give their interpretive responses (the subtext). They will say things like: "At the beginning, Serri was embarrassed," "Bill was overconfident and angry." Once the **Two**s have completed their interpretation of the puzzle-makers' feelings, ask the volunteers if the **Two**s were right in their responses. (You wouldn't ask the **One**s because the actions (facts) spoke for themselves.) You will be able to have an interesting discussion on which body language or action might lead a **Two** to interpret accurately or inaccurately. There will be misinterpretations, but the responses of your Living Short Story characters should be truthful.

- Ask, "Which was more interesting – listening to the **One**s or **Two**s? Why?" Students quickly realize that comprehending and interpreting subtext are more fun and exciting than knowing the text.

- This workshop will work well across the curriculum. Students can discover just as much subtext in a passage from a history textbook as in a short story.

Allusions

Teacher Preparation: Prepare a list of the allusions contained in a passage of material so that you can give each small group of students a copy of the list.

Classroom Preparation: Each group will need access to dictionaries, encyclopedias, books of quotations, mythology reference works, and perhaps other reference books; therefore, if you do not have these available in your classroom, you might want to take your class to the library for this workshop.

Length of Time: The time will depend on how many allusions you give the students.

• Authors often refer to persons, places, and events from mythology, religion, literature, history, etc., in order to enhance their subject. Many of these allusions, however, can pass students by and leave them ignorant of why the author introduced this or that strange word.

• Use this workshop for passages of your course material which contain many allusions. Or you might use an article from a popular magazine or even the sports page of your local newspaper to show that writers use allusions without apology and that readers who don't appreciate the writer's references will only understand a portion of the article.

• Through discussion and searching, students should find each allusion and determine why the author introduced it into the passage. Having them report their findings within a full class discussion will ensure that allusions become an important part of every student's life.

• As a variation, you might give each group a different set of allusions.

Visual-allusion Treasure Hunt

• Because cartoons, advertisements, and other visual material often contain allusions, start gathering them from magazines and newspapers. As well, ask your students to add to your collection.

• After you have collected 25 or so, number each and place them all around the room for a Visual Allusion Treasure Hunt. Give students a piece of paper with corresponding numbers and ask them, over the next week, to explain the allusion in each cartoon, advertisement, or picture. They should not discuss their findings with anyone else. During the week, they can use all the resources of the school's library to seek an explanation for the allusions.

• As a follow-up, give students an opportunity to share their findings about each allusion. If no one is able to explain an allusion in the material, you will have a rapt audience as you point out the allusion.

Twenty-Five-Word Comprehension Summary

Teacher Preparation: None required.

Length of Time: 5 to 10 minutes to evaluate the summaries.

• After students experience a long passage of material (a chapter of a textbook, for example), ask them to bring to class the next day a summary of the passage in *exactly* 25 words so that the reader will understand the purpose, significance, or importance of the passage. The summary should not be a mere retelling of the content (knowledge). Encourage students to mention the title and author's name of the passage, but let them know that these will not be counted in the 25 words. (See "Twenty-Five-Word Knowledge Summary" in the previous chapter for more details.)

- When students come with their 25-word summaries, have them post them around the room for everyone's evaluation, or have them form small groups to evaluate them. Have them choose one they think best interprets the *subtext* and present it to the rest of the class. During a class discussion, students can determine which 25-word summary shows the best comprehension of the passage of material.

Testing Communication Skills

Teacher Preparation: None required.
Classroom Preparation: Set up an inner and outer circle of desks.
Length of Time: As long as the original workshop takes.

- While one group is participating in a workshop, assign another group to sit around the group as observers. Assign each student in the outer group to observe a particular student in the inner group (but do not tell the members of the inner group who is observing whom). The task of each member of the outer group is to write down not only everything that the assigned inner-group member says and does but an interpretation of his/her actions: asks questions, answers questions, dominates, does not speak, changes the subject, does not take part, sabotages discussion, etc. Thus, the students in the outer circle record both.the text and subtext of the discussion.
- After the workshop, in a one-to-one session, the students from the outer circle discuss their findings with those from the inner circle. Encourage the evaluators to suggest ways for the inner group to improve their communication skills.
- At a later date, repeat the test, but make sure that none of the observers has the same partner as during the first testing.

The Comprehension Envelope, Please

- Use this workshop in exactly the same way as "The Knowledge Envelope, Please" in Chapter 17, except that students will use the comprehension key words in this chapter to compose their 20 questions.

IDEAS FOR COMPREHENSION WORKSHOPS

CHAPTER NINETEEN

Analysis

When analyzing, students not only see how the pieces of a body of learned material fit together, but can also examine each piece to determine its relationship to the others. Once students have successfully analyzed the material, they are ready to use it in real and meaningful projects through application, evaluation, and synthesis.

Each piece of knowledge and comprehension is in itself unimportant; only when we interlock the pieces to make a whole picture do we become interested in learning. At the same time, though, analysis should lead students to more relevant, exciting higher-level thinking strategies.

The following workshops help students analyze written, visual or aural material, but they are also stepping stones to other thinking strategies. Adapt them to fit your grade and subject matter; extend and blend them to encourage application, evaluation, and synthesis. In order for students to have opportunities to question, make sure that all groups are small – no more than four. Visiting groups and including follow-up discussion sessions will ensure that all students have discovered relevant information to back up their analysis and now understand and appreciate the importance of developing their analytical skills.

Key Words to Stimulate Analysis

Teacher Preparation: Prepare a three-part analysis question based on a passage of material for demonstration purposes. Make an overhead transparency of the Analysis Key Words, boxed in Chapter 2.
Length of Time: 20 minutes.

- Encourage students to make up questions using the following key words as outlined in Chapter Six: **divide, break down, dissect, identify, point out, differentiate, find the difference between, compare, contrast, compare and contrast, discover relevant information, show the cause, effect, cause and effect, or effect and cause, classify, categorize, group, compile, arrange, outline, illustrate visually, draw, diagram.**
- As a follow-up, evaluate their questions in a class discussion. Help the evaluation by asking questions like, "Is there a key word or words in the question? What is the object of the question? What is the limiting factor? Will the answerer know exactly what to analyze?"
- Duplicate the following example or make up your own:

Three-part Analysis Question

"Compare the conditions that caused British Columbia to become part of Canada in 1871 to those that caused Newfoundland's entry in 1949."

Key Word:	compare
Object:	to look for similarities between BC and Newfoundland in the reasons each became part of Canada.
Limiting Factor:	examine conditions before 1871 in BC and before 1949 in Newfoundland.

Break Down

Teacher Preparation: None required.

- To help students see all the parts of a piece of material, choose something that you want them to break down by dividing, dissecting, identifying, pointing out, classifying, categorizing, grouping, compiling, arranging, or outlining. You can give them specific instructions or allow them to break down the material as they see fit in order to determine how the parts fit into the whole. Through questioning each other and using the key words, students will become more familiar with the analysis terms.
- In English classes, students can learn to divide sentences into dependent and independent clauses; point out the parts of speech of each word in a sentence; identify the different parts of a short story; classify the characters in a play as protagonists, antagonists, or neutrals. The list of analysis "break down" questions in English classes can go on forever. I expect that the same is true for most other subjects: divide chemical compounds into their elements; point out all the countries in Africa on a map; dissect a frog and identify its parts; classify the hierarchy in the Cabinet.

YOUR OWN BREAK-DOWN IDEAS

- Either you can give students a Break-Down Analysis question or groups can make up their own. Then, they can perform the analysis within small groups, come to a consensus, discuss their analysis within a class discussion, and prepare to go on to the next level of learning: application.

Tasks to Differentiate

Teacher Preparation: If you have material that requires students to see both halves, focus on the more specific analysis terms below.

- To help students see the relationship between different parts of a piece of material, choose something that contains distinctly different parts so that they can find the differences between the parts, compare and contrast them, point out causes and effects, reasons and results. You can give them specific instructions or allow them to work on their own to differentiate between the parts in order to determine how the parts relate to each other.
- In English classes, students can work to find the effects of using active or passive voice, contrast the hero and villain in a movie, discover the causes of a protagonist's actions, provide the effects of an antagonist's actions, list the results of having an essay peer edited, point out the differences between peer editing and teacher editing. The list of analysis "differentiate" questions in English classes can go on forever. I expect that the same is true for most other subjects: for example, show the effect of adding one particular chemical to another chemical; contrast life in Russia in the 1960s with life there in the 1990s; list the results of our Open House.

YOUR OWN DIFFERENTIATE TASKS

- Either you can give students a Differentiate Analysis question or groups can make up their own. Then, they can perform the analysis within small groups, come to a consensus by perhaps blending this workshop with one of the problem-solving workshops (Chapter 13), and discuss their analysis within a class discussion.

Illustrate Visually

Teacher Preparation: Single out passages of material that lend themselves to analysis through visual illustrations.

- To help students visualize a piece of written material, choose one that lends itself to their drawing, charting, graphing, or diagramming.
- English teachers have devised numerous visual aids to help students see the parts of sentences: single lines under subjects, double lines under predicates, triple under objects, circles around phrases, arrows drawn from adjectives to words they modify, etc. As well, annotated graphs often bring the parts of a novel or play into perspective: rising action, crisis, climax, anti-climax, dénouement. (See Brainstorming with Graphics, Chapter Eight for more details.) Most other subjects lend themselves to analysis through visual illustrations even better than English. For example, students can illustrate fractions visually using a pie chart, use a bar graph to show the rate of growth of a country's economy, or draw diagrams to show the step-by-step process of a particular physical exercise.

YOUR OWN IDEAS FOR VISUAL ILLUSTRATIONS

- Either you can give students an analysis question that will lead to a visual illustration or groups can make up their own. Then, they can execute the graphic within small groups, come to a consensus, and display their graphics for the rest of the class to enjoy and evaluate. As a variation, you may have several graphics in your course material that need analysis. Reversing the above process, students will need to talk about the parts of the graphic to see how they fit together to make the diagram, graph, or other visual illustration.

Up/Down; One Up

Teacher Preparation: Just assign after you've completed a unit of material.
Length of Time: 20 minutes.

- To test analysis, divide a large amount of material into workable units. Assign each unit to a group of students.
- The group of students should become the experts and draw up a number of analysis questions on the material. The rest of the class divide into groups of five, standing in circles. Just clear the desks to the sides of the room. After all the groups are standing in circles, the experts present the first question.
- When *everyone* in a group knows the answer, the entire group sits down on the floor. They are not allowed to discuss anything once they've sat down. When all groups are sitting, the experts choose one person from the group that sat down first to answer their question. That person stands to answer. If the answer is correct, that group gets a point and the experts ask another question. If the answer is incorrect, the experts asks one person from the second group that sat down. (The experts figure out the order of who sat first, ensure that no sitting group discusses the answer, etc.)
- This workshop works well after a Jigsawing workshop (Chapter 11), a Post-viewing workshop (Chapter 16), or after reading a chapter from a textbook. To fit your needs, you will probably think of other ways to use this very active-learning workshop.

Analysis Examinations

Teacher Preparation: Compose a "bare bones" exam along the lines of the one illustrated in "Student-Conceived Exams" in Chapter 6.
Length of Time: As long as you wish. See details in Chapter 6.

- Instead of your making up final examinations, encourage students to make up analysis exams for other students. After completing a unit of material, ask students to bring to the exam a completed "bare bones" exam. They must make sure that their analysis question contains an analysis key word, an object, and a limiting factor. Also, they must put their name on the exam in the space provided.
- On the day of the exam, collect all "bare bones" exams. Place them face down at the front of the room. Invite students to choose one. For three or four minutes they may confer with the "examiner" about the analysis question. If the examiner agrees to change the question, he/she must amend the question on the paper accordingly. Students can then spend the rest of the time completing the analysis exam. For marking and grading suggestions, see Chapter 5.
- For their first analysis exam, suggest a simple question that will require only fifteen minutes to answer. For example, ask them to
  - compare the boundaries of the Iron Curtain at the beginning of 1989 and today
  - differentiate between the properties of methane and ammonia
  - contrast the sports featured in the original Olympic Games with those in today's Olympics
- What do you think of the student-composed Analysis Exam on the next page? You can adapt it to fit your needs.

Analysis Exam   _____
                                                        (name)

Read the following poem and paragraph chosen by _____.

Loveliest of Trees, the Cherry Now
        by. A. E. Housman

Loveliest of trees, the cherry now
Is hung with bloom along the bough,
And stands about the woodland ride
Wearing white for Eastertide.

Now, of my threescore years and ten,
Twenty will not come again,
And take from seventy springs a score,
It only leaves me fifty more.

And since to look at things in bloom
Fifty springs are little room,
About the woodlands I will go
To see the cherry hung with snow.

                Snow
from *Flames Across the Border* by Pierre Berton

Snow. Snow falling in a curtain of heavy flakes. Snow blowing in the teeth
of a bitter east wind off the lake. Snow lying calf deep in the streets, whirling
in eddies around log buildings, creeping under doors, piling in drifts at the
base of snake fences.

With specific reference to the text, write an analysis – on separate paper – in
response to the following question:
Find the difference between each writer's feelings about snow and write about
the different *effects* snow has on him.

- On the day of the exam, have a few analysis topics already composed in case a
  student comes without one. (That student doesn't get to choose; instead, he or
  she does yours.) If you discover during the first three or four minutes that
  someone is having difficulty dealing with a poorly worded student-composed
  question, you might like to give him/her one of yours. Don't be concerned if
  several students are unable to compose appropriate questions the first time
  around; next time they will do better.
- The benefits of student-composed exams are many:
    - they help students learn to ask worthwhile questions
    - they create a stronger classroom learning community
    - they are much more interesting to mark and grade – something new on
      every paper!
    - if you decide to have the "examiners" mark and grade the exams, you
      will have new-found freedom

Unconventional Analysis Techniques

Teacher Preparation: Decide after you read the following.

• Over the centuries, humans have developed many techniques that supposedly give insight into character. None of these is infallibly valid; however, you might want to have students use one or more of them to see what they can discover about actual or fictional characters.

Plato-analysis – using Plato's idea that humans are driven through life by physical and spiritual forces, students can analyze a character to determine whether he/she is ruled more by physical or spiritual needs

Psycho-analysis – using Freud's divisions of personality into id, ego, and superego, students can analyze characters, perhaps dividing a pie chart into sections corresponding to how much of each aspect of personality they think each character displays.

Aggression-analysis – using Freud's psychoanalytical terms (denial, projection, repression, displacement, displaced aggression, reaction formation, and aggressive phase), students can analyze a character

Jung-analysis – using Carl Jung's theories, students can analyze characters in how they relate to their conscious and unconscious actions and in how they are extroverted or introverted. In addition, they can identify the personal unconscious (repressed feelings) and the collective unconscious (inherited feelings, thoughts, and memories shared by all humanity).

Archetypal-analysis – using Jung's theories of archetype, students can examine characters in terms of the archetypal experience or situation in which they find themselves, the archetypal conflict they are enduring, and the archetypal character they identify with.

Conflict-analysis – students should look closely at the *specific* conflict a character is involved in (either a piece of literature or a real-life situation). Then, they should stand back from it and see the *larger* conflict (battle of the sexes, generation gap, love, race, religion, etc.)

Campbell-analysis – using Joseph Campbell's myths to live by, students can link a character to a myth and reflect on how the character fits into and copes with society.

Erikson-analysis – using Erik Erikson's achievement scale of personality formation, students can contrast different aspects of a character: trusts/mistrusts, autonomous/doubting, initiative/guilt, industrious/inferior, identity/role confusion, intimate with losing identity/isolation, creatively productive/negative self-absorption, peace of mind integrity/despair. Because Erikson believes that change is possible, students can note changes that have taken place in the character.

Rogers-analysis – using Carl Rogers' ideas that individuals are unique and that pigeonholing is unnecessary, students can analyze a character in terms of self-actualization and how the character shapes his/her own world and perceives him/herself in that world.

Maslow-analysis – using Maslow's hierarchy of motives – physiological (food, water, oxygen), safety (nurture, money), belonging and love (acceptance, affection), esteem (self respect), and self-actualization (maximizing one's potential), students can determine a character's motives.

IQ-analysis – using one of the many standardized IQ tests, students might anticipate a character's score and determine his/her mental age (as well as noting the character's chronological age). In addition, students can analyze how various outside stimuli might affect the IQ results: environment, ethnic origin, birth order, love and affection, etc.

Political-analysis – using the *isms* (liberalism, conservatism, communism, totalitarianism, fascism, primitivism, Maoism, etc.), students should find evidence to determine a character's political beliefs.

Religious-analysis – using the various religions (Christianity, Judaism, Hinduism, Islam, Atheism, Agnosticism, etc.), students should find evidence to determine a character's religious beliefs.

Creative-analysis – students might determine how creative or non-creative a character is and how this knowledge affects what the character does.

Ancestor-analysis – students can look into the background of a character in order to create a family tree and determine how the character's ancestors have affected him/her.

Work-analysis – examining a character's attitude toward the work ethic might help explain the actions of a character.

Astro-analysis – the sign of the zodiac under which a character is "born" supposedly provides insight into character.

Numer-analysis – according to believers, the numerical value of a person's or character's name, computed by any of various systems, can show what sort of person the character is.

- Students should have no trouble finding books about any of the above techniques if they need more information.
- Feel free to modify these as you see fit or add to them; for example, students might look at a character in terms of kindness/wickedness, giver/taker, honest/dishonest, courage/coward, rich/poor, etc. There are 150 different types of mental processes to analyze characters.

IDEAS FOR ANALYSIS WORKSHOPS

CHAPTER TWENTY

Application

To keep students eagerly learning, teachers must make their courses relevant to students' needs. Students who see no relevance in their courses, who are convinced that one course has nothing to do with any others, who think that their teachers' sole purpose is to keep them busily working only to improve their grades, soon become disenchanted with education and cannot wait for the day that they can get out into the world and **really** start learning. By taking part in active-learning workshops and applying what they learn in one class to what they are learning in other classes, to what they have already learned, to what they have yet to learn, and to their own experiences, talents, and interests, students will find their education enriching.

From their first day, you should endeavor to help your students find a reason for taking your course. Even though students primarily want to know what's on the reading list and what assignments they have to do, the first sentence in your course outline should deal with the purpose and objectives of the course: for example, "The objective of English 230 is to help you become independent thinkers, readers, writers, and viewers....I have chosen the novels, poetry, and films and designed the workshops, activities, assignments, and examinations, to help you achieve this objective." I suggest they should open their minds for changes to occur within their own lives — a synthesis — as a result of meeting not only new pieces of literature but also new experiences and new people within their new learning community.

Key Words to Stimulate Application

Teacher Preparation: Prepare a sample three-part application question for demonstration purposes, as well as putting the Application Key Words (boxed in Chapter 2) on a transparency.
Length of Time: 20 minutes.

- Suggest that students use the following key words as outlined in Chapter Six, to make up application questions: **imagine, pretend, make believe, visualize, put yourself in the situation of, use your knowledge to, suppose, assume.**
- After students have composed several application questions, evaluate them by conducting a class discussion. Let the students apply what they have heard you do in your evaluation of the Knowledge, Comprehension, and Analysis questions from the previous chapters.
- Duplicate the following example or make up one of your own:

Three-part Application Question

"Use your knowledge of Hitler's strategies to suggest how he lost World War II."

Key Words:	use your knowledge of
Object:	to determine how Hitler lost World War II.
Limiting Factors:	knowledge of Hitler's strategies in fighting and planning World War II.

Note: Application and Synthesis

Some of the application key words, especially "pretend" and "imagine," may inspire students to create synthesis questions, in which the answer consists of a new product based on combining several aspects of their experience and knowledge. But whereas synthesis can create products bounded only by imagination, application is limited to what students can know, understand, and analyze. A cook, for example, can apply knowledge of cooking and follow a recipe to turn out the same delicious product every time; as well, she or he can use the original recipe, as well as experience and imagination, to create a completely new dish – a synthesis. Another example to help students discover the difference between application and synthesis involves the career of Joseph Conrad. When he decided to become a writer, he knew almost no English. In order to learn both English and the art of writing, so the story goes, he copied the works of Robert Louis Stevenson, and learned by application. Because of this learning method, his early writing greatly resembled Stevenson's. His later work, however, demonstrates a synthesis of a new and very successful style, a blend of Stevenson and his own genius and experiences.

Best Subject/Worst Subject

Teacher Preparation: None required.
Length of Time: 15 minutes.

- To determine how much experience students have had with application thinking, have students get into small groups. Have them share their best and worst educational experiences – they might deal with an entire subject or a single course. They do not, however, need to name names. Once they have shared their best and worst educational experiences, have one person from each group record the reasons why the best experience was best and the worst one was worst.

- In a follow-up discussion session, listen for reasons that reflect application thinking. Emphasize the fact in your comments that students will have plenty of opportunities to apply what they learn in your class to real and imagined situations. If, next term, another instructor presents this same workshop, perhaps your students will then put your course into the "best" category!

Imagination

Teacher Preparation: None required.
Length of Time: 20 to 30 minutes.

- After having completed a unit of course content (students know, understand, and have analyzed it), have students form small groups.
- Ask them to use one of the following key words to make up an imaginative application topic for another group of students: *pretend, make believe, put yourself in the situation of, suppose, assume*. They must make sure that their topic will encourage the other students to use their imaginations. You might give them a couple of sample topics to get them thinking, pointing out the key words, object, and limiting factor.
- For example, you might present a topic similar to one of these:
  - "If South Africa had a black president, how would life be different both for black South Africans and for others? Use your knowledge of South Africa to say what might change immediately and what might not change for some time, perhaps years. Discuss this within groups and be prepared to present your group's thoughts to the class."
  - "Each member of the group should pretend that he or she is a big-time Hollywood producer with an unlimited budget. Specific instructions: 'You want to film **the novel that we have just finished studying**. Write the author a letter which includes an offer, an explanation of how you would film the novel, whom you would cast in the leading roles, where you would film it, what theme you would emphasize in your production, and anything else that you think necessary in order to convince the author to give you the film rights. When you all finish your letters, share them to determine the most effective one. Be prepared to present the best one to the whole class.'"
- For other courses across the curriculum, Imagination workshops can expand students' appreciation of the course content as well as helping them see the relevancy of having to learn the material. Such Imagination questions will do wonders and inject new life into humdrum material: "Imagine that you could travel in time (like Michael J. Fox in the *Back to the Future* movies), and you have an opportunity to convince Napoleon not to invade Russia. What would you say to him?" "Assume that you have to teach this course next term; how would you teach it?" "Put yourself ten years in the future. Which parts of the body of material we have just completed will you find indispensable? Why will this information be important to you?"

YOUR OWN IMAGINATION IDEAS

Prediction

Teacher Preparation: If you find your students are not involved with your course, prepare small-group discussions, using the material below.

- In order for students to become active learners, it's important that they spend a bit of time predicting what will happen next in a text, a novel, or even in the classroom. We predict naturally when we read or see a mystery; we are constantly trying to discover "Who dun it?" Using the same strategies, students can become actively involved in what they are learning. You might ask students to stop three or four times while reading a novel and predict what they think will happen to the main characters, how the conflict will be resolved, what the climax will be. Or while reading their textbook, students can predict the outcome of the material. Ask students to write their predictions in their journals so that when they finish reading, they can check to see how accurately they have predicted. Such an exercise helps students focus on the clues that authors give to help their readers become actively involved.
- Within discussion groups, encourage students to use their knowledge of the material they have recently learned to predict
  - what will happen in the next unit of material
  - how they will use it in another course
  - how it will help them in the future
  - what could be on the next exam

Application Exams

Teacher Preparation: Ask students to make up application questions for other students. For procedural information, see the Analysis chapter.

- For their first application exam, suggest a simple assignment that requires only 10 minutes to complete. For example, after studying the Shakespearean sonnet, suggest that students find a suitable sonnet and compose a simple application topic. You might suggest the following one: "After studying the accompanying Shakespearean sonnet and using your knowledge of the characteristics of the sonnet, compose a new final couplet. Make sure that it fits the content, rhythm, rhyme, and overall style of the original sonnet."
- Application exams work well for courses across the curriculum; for example, "Assume that you are living in the Soviet Union. How would your life be different from that of someone your age in North America?" "Using your knowledge of the effects of earthquakes, predict what damage might occur in your school if an earthquake measuring 6 on the Richter scale took place." "Now that you know, understand, and have analyzed the Pythagorean Theorem, use it to solve three geometry problems."
- See Chapters 6 for more practical suggestions on composing exam questions.

Mock Trial

Teacher Preparation: After students have become familiar with a body of
   course content, assign groups of four the task of creating a Mock Trial.
Student Preparation: Members of each group, working together, should choose a
   "crime" for which a "defendant" can be put on trial; then prepare one bag
   for each of the other groups in the class, containing an envelope with
   instructions to allow each group member to play a role in the trial, along
   with props, costume pieces, and other material to help the trial proceed.
Length of Time: 5 to 8 minutes per trial.

* On the day of the Mock Trial, have students get into their original groups.
  Taking turns, the members of each group should present their "crime" by
  giving the other groups a prepared bag.
* Before the Mock Trial, the organizing group give each of the other groups a
  bag with these instructions: "Open the envelope first and each select one of the
  folded pieces of paper to find out which part you play in the trial. You are not
  allowed to tell others what is on your paper other than what part you will take
  in the trial."
* To help them prepare for the trials, the originating group members should
  move from trial to trial acting as facilitators. Each group will conduct a
  separate trial.
* The organizing group times each phase of the Mock Trial accordingly:

   Prosecuting Attorney: one minute
   Defense Attorney: one minute
   Defendant: one minute
   Free for all: one and a half minutes
   Judge's deliberation: one minute.

* As a follow-up, since all groups are trying the same Defendant, discuss any
  disagreements in the "verdicts" rendered by the Judges.
* Read how one group conducted a Mock Trial based on *The Handmaid's Tale*
  (the trial took place at the time when the novel was set – 2015).

   Prosecuting Attorney – You are a fundamentalist. You feel that with so
      many women unable to bear children, abortion is wrong. Some other
      arguments against the Defendant may be: (1) God is against abortion; it
      is evil. (2) Women were put on this earth to bear children; it is their
      purpose in life. (3) Abortion is another contributing factor to the world's
      population decline. You must wear the armband signifying that you are
      also an "Eye." Do not bring up the argument of the fetus's rights; this is
      not the issue.
   Defense Attorney – You must hold strong views about equal rights. Some
      of your arguments to justify the Defendant's actions may be: (1)
      Women's rights must be taken into consideration. (2) The physical and
      mental health and welfare of the mother may be at stake. (3) The mother
      was raped and, as a result, became pregnant. You must wear the paper
      bag over your head for your own security.   There are staunch
      fundamentalists viewing the trial who may later make an attempt on
      your life.
   Defendant – You have performed an abortion but you feel it was your duty
      to the woman. During the trial you may be asked questions by both the
      Prosecuting Attorney and your attorney. Defend your actions. You
      must wear the white coat and the purple placard with a fetus around your
      neck. Briefly discuss with your attorney your plan of action prior to the
      start of the trial.

Judge – You are responsible to listen to the arguments for and against the Defendant's performing an abortion. After, you must decide whether the Defendant is guilty or innocent. If guilty, you must decide if he/she is to be sent to the colonies or is to die on the wall. Remember, you are a judge in Gilead, not in your present-day society. You should use the hammer in the bag as a gavel. (If the group has five or more members, have more than one Judge.)

Application through Roleplaying

Teacher Preparation: See Chapter Thirteen for full details on how to conduct roleplaying sessions.

Length of Time: No more than 10 minutes at the beginning of a few periods.

• You might want students – under your guidance – to engage in several roleplaying workshops, to apply their own situations to the course content. See Chapter Thirteen for details about roleplaying.

SPECIFIC IDEAS FOR APPLICATION ROLEPLAYING

CHAPTER TWENTY-ONE

Evaluation

Every day we face choices: Should I get out of bed or roll over and go back to sleep? Should I apply for this job or that one? Should I begin a pension fund? Which car should I buy? One sign of maturity is being able to make evaluative decisions.

By introducing students to decision-making exercises in their courses, teachers help to prepare them for life decisions. Giving students the tools to make informed choices is perhaps one of the most essential tasks that teachers can perform.

Once students know and understand a portion of course content, let them try their hand at evaluating it in a variety of workshops.

Key Words to Stimulate Evaluation

Teacher Preparation: Compose a three-part Evaluation question for demonstration purposes, and put the Evaluation Key Words (boxed in Chapter 2) on a transparency.
Length of Time: 20 minutes.

- When you want students to evaluate, give them this list of key words and encourage them to make up questions as outlined in Chapter 6: **rank, order, judge, grade, measure, assess, appraise, discriminate, distinguish between, select, determine, decide, support, explain, critique, criticize, recommend, suggest, convince, persuade**.
- After students have composed a number of evaluation questions, gather them up and have the class rank them. Through discussion, you will find out whether they need to work further on composing useful three-part Evaluation questions.
- Duplicate the following example or make up one yourself:

Three-part Evaluation Question

"According to the number of safety-related features each contains, determine which compact car is safest to drive."

Key Word:	determine
Object:	to find out which compact car is safest to drive
Limiting Factors:	cars must be compact
	only safety-related features to be examined

Rank

Teacher Preparation: Focus on material that you wish students to rank.

- This workshop allows students to order, judge, grade, measure, assess, appraise, discriminate, distinguish between, and select parts of course content. Applying judgments of course content to other parts of the course, other courses, and their own life experiences will make the workshop even more meaningful and worthwhile for students.
- After learning a body of material, students may use the key words to ask their own evaluative questions, or you may assign questions yourself. Here are some examples of evaluation questions:
  - Within your group, list as many novels, films, plays, and TV productions as you can that deal with a look into the future. For anything on the list that is unfamiliar, the student who suggested the selection should outline its plot and main purpose. Spend a few minutes to rank each item from the one the group thinks works best to the one that works least best. Be prepared to back up your ranking with plenty of support. Share your list and reasons for your ranking order with the rest of the class.
  - Since we have become more concerned about the effects of many products and processes on the environment, manufacturers have begun to market so-called "green" or "environmentally friendly" products. Some of these are new; some are already-existing products repackaged to make them appear environmentally beneficial. Choose ten of these products available on local supermarket shelves and rank them from most to least "environmentally friendly." What criteria will you use? If you think a product on your list might not benefit the environment, consider asking the supermarket to stop carrying the product.
- The last question clearly links course content with events outside the classroom. Linking application and evaluation in the same workshop makes the project more relevant.

YOUR OWN RANKING IDEAS

Argue

Teacher Preparation: Use the following suggestions with material that requires students to take a strong stand.

- This workshop allows students to persuade, convince, determine, decide, recommend, suggest, support, and explain parts of course content. Applying course content to other parts of the course, other courses, and their own life experiences will make the workshop even more meaningful and worthwhile for students.
- After learning a body of material, students may use the key words to ask their own evaluative questions or you may assign questions yourself. For example, here is a workshop idea based on Margaret Atwood's *The Handmaid's Tale*:
    - Form groups of five or more. Each group member should choose a different job found in the society of Gilead: Commander, Wife, Handmaid, Aunt, Eye, Guardian, etc. Rank the jobs as to their importance in Gilead, but place your job first since you must consider it most important. Once you have ranked the jobs, convince the others in your group that your order has merit. Provide plenty of support for your argument. When you have finished your argument, take a secret ballot to make a new ranking, based on the group discussion. During the vote, you are not allowed to vote for yourself. Present your results to the rest of the class for discussion.
    - In pairs, students should argue whether a particular portion of course content they have already studied should or should not be part of the curriculum. The older student must argue in favor of the material; the younger, against it. After five minutes, they must choose a winner. In a follow-up, find out how many students are in favor of including the material and how many are against it. If the majority of students see no relevance to the material, you can work either on making it more relevant or on eliminating it from the curriculum.
- After composing a product (poem, essay, or any other written or visual product), form groups of four or five. Apply the suggestions as above. Present the best product to the whole class. The whole class might evaluate the products of each presenter.

YOUR OWN ARGUMENT IDEAS

Critique

Teacher Preparation: Use the instructions below when you have material that requires critiquing.

- Hardly a day goes by when we are not asked to criticize. What did you think of last night's movie? How did you like that class? Do I look better in blue eyeshadow or brown? Wouldn't it be easier and faster to use a calculator than my head?
- Providing workshops for students to criticize course content will help them distinguish between what works well and what doesn't work well, will prove to them that worthwhile support for their decisions is necessary, and will allow them to practice making decisions in real-life critical situations.
- Provide a list of statements based on a portion of your course content. Ask students to write next to each statement "agree" or "disagree." When they have finished, ask them to compare their responses with those of others. They should find one student who agrees with them on at least one statement. The pair of students should get together to gather as much support as they can for the statement that they agree on. They are going to work together as a solid team in complete agreement on that one statement. Afterwards, they should find another pair who disagree with them on that statement. Each pair should take turns to present their position on the statement. Afterwards, they should try to convince the other pair that they are wrong. During a follow-up, pairs should report their victories.
- Here is a list of statements I've given my literature students:
  - *1984* is a better novel than *The Handmaid's Tale*.
  - *The Handmaid's Tale* is a better novel than *1984* .
  - Offred escapes from Gilead.
  - Offred does not escape from Gilead.
  - The Commander is impotent.
  - The Commander is not impotent.
  - Luke is still alive.
  - Luke is dead.
  - *Handmaid's* is Atwood's best novel to date.
  - *Handmaid's* is not Atwood's best novel to date.

Stars Up

Teacher Preparation: Make a series of one-, two-, three- and four-star cards so that each group of four students has one set of cards.

- This workshop works well for groups to evaluate the quality of a unit of material.
- After showing a film, for example, give each group a set of cards. Ask all groups to evaluate the photography of the film and arrive at a consensus. After they discuss their evaluation, ask a representative from each group to raise one of the cards (one star for below average, two stars for so-so, three stars for above average, and four stars for outstanding). Record each decision. If one or two are far away from the majority, ask them to justify their decisions. Then, ask each group to evaluate the acting, direction, costumes, and so on.
- You can use Stars Up to evaluate essays (Content, Organization, Style, Mechanics), scientific labs, mathematical problems, paintings, etc.

Evaluations of Exams

• As outlined in the last two chapters and Chapter 6, you can have students evaluate exams that they have composed for other students.

Evaluations of Presentations

Teacher Preparation: Make up an evaluation form.

• Instead of being the only evaluator of your students' active-learning presentations, consider choosing four students at random, giving them copies of an evaluation form, and having them evaluate the presentations too. Combine their evaluations with yours and give all five to the presenters after their workshop. When presenters receive five evaluations instead of one, they have a better idea of how they did.
• Duplicate or modify this evaluation form to fit your needs:

Anonymous Evaluation Form

Subject of Presentation _____

Presenters _____   _____   _____

_____   _____   _____

I would give you _____ marks out of 10 for your presentation.

SPECIFIC COMMENTS TO JUSTIFY MY MARK:
Things that worked well:

Things that needed more attention:

For your next presentation, I suggest you work on

IDEAS FOR MORE EVALUATION WORKSHOPS

CHAPTER TWENTY-TWO

Synthesis

Many teachers and students believe that the best way to test knowledge and understanding is to have students write a clear essay or complete a successful examination. By suggesting, however, that students synthesize what they know about the course content with something else that they know in order to produce a new, original product, you will raise students' higher-level thinking skills, allow them to make their products relevant to their lives and the real world, and ensure unique and outstanding results. By encouraging students to blend two or more of their courses, you help them to see that their *total* education is important.

The products of synthesis can be minor or major: essays, comic strips, cartoons, video presentations, film scripts, skits, short plays, songs, board games, crossword puzzles, dialogues, debates, slide shows, audio cassettes, class publications, contests, proposals, reports, brochures, lesson plans, letters to the editor...in fact, almost anything. Occasionally, you might give an assignment free of format restrictions, allowing students to choose any format they wish to display their knowledge, understanding, and appreciation of a part of the course. Other times, you might like to group students and have them collectively work in a particular format.

In this section of *Workshops for Active Learning*, you will discover various ways in which you might help your students synthesize the content from your course with the content of their own lives or that of one or more of their other courses. (By the way, many new programs of study in our schools are a result of synthesis thinking: for example, Pacific Rim Studies, Women's Studies, Peace Program, Ecology Department, etc. Students in these programs find that they are constantly synthesizing two or more of their courses rather than studying each course by itself.)

Key Words to Stimulate Synthesis

Teacher Preparation: Produce a three-part Synthesis question for
    demonstration purposes, and then duplicate the Synthesis Key Words
    (boxed in Chapter 2) on a transparency.
Length of Time: 20 minutes.

- Give students the following key words to think about as they synthesize to create an original product: **combine, integrate, modify, revise, improve, rearrange, reconstruct, substitute, create, generate, devise, design, compose, plan, predict, estimate, hypothesize.** As a follow-up, let students evaluate the synthesis questions in order to make sure that each contains a key word, an object, and a limiting factor.
- Duplicate the following example or make up one of your own:

Three-part Synthesis Question

"Rearrange the amendments to the U.S. Constitution in order from least to most important in everyday life. As well, devise any new amendments that you think would improve everyday life."

Key Words:	rearrange and devise
Object:	to discover which constitutional amendments you consider most important and which you would like to add to improve everyday life
Limiting Factor:	deal only with amendments to the U.S. constitution

---

Moving from One Written Format to Another

Teacher Preparation: None required.
Length of Time: As much as you please.

- By demonstrating their ability to synthesize material, students will show that they have not only a keen understanding of the course content but also a better appreciation of it. So that students always have a sense of adaptability, provide abundant opportunities for them to blend learned material into various genres.
- Instead of routinely assigning a typical term paper at the end of a unit of material, occasionally suggest that students write in a different genre. For example, have them write a short story based on a period that they are studying in their history course, using invented characters as well as a few actual historical characters. After reviewing the qualities of a short story (single plot, initial incident, crisis, conflict, suspense, climax, resolution, dialogue, etc.), students will be able to use information both from the historical period and from their imaginations. The results will be entertaining and beneficial and will beg to be shared with both the history and English classes.
- For more ambitious projects, you might like to assign an epic. (See "Traditions" in Chapter 12.) "Choose one of the historical personalities you have studied so far this year and make that person the hero of a 250-line epic."
- There really is no end to the possibilities of synthesis. Once you get started, you will come up with ideas you never thought of before. Here are just a few to get you thinking of ways to use a variety of formats to synthesize your course material:
  - write a letter to a friend who plans to take this course next term. Explain the best way to pass.
  - write a limerick about photosynthesis
  - write a script for TV so that viewers will understand and appreciate the portion of material we have just studied.
  - write a dialogue with conflict between Freud and yourself
  - make up a radio commercial to "sell" the idea of angles in geometry.
  - compose a sonnet on the life of Picasso

YOUR OWN IDEAS FOR WRITTEN SYNTHESIS PROJECTS

Boil Down

Teacher Preparation: None needed.
Length of Time: 4 to 5 minutes.

- Asking students to boil down the raw material of a course into a useful, usable form that they can carry away from the classroom should prove beneficial. If, in addition, they can blend their findings with a memorable device, they might retain the information forever.
- In the following group of workshops, ask students to design, compose, plan, create, generate, or devise a new product by blending at least two things they already know. Use these workshops in connection with students' remembering facts, details, reasons, etc.

Couplet

- No matter the course or grade level, encourage all students, after they have completed a lengthy project, to synthesize the object, theory, main idea, or purpose into a memorable couplet. If students are particularly ambitious, ask that the couplet be in iambic pentameter or alexandrines. And if they wish more of a challenge, ask them for a rhyming couplet.
- On completion of the couplets, make sure that all students are able to hear or read all products. Posting them around the room will do the trick. Students will often copy down outstanding couplets in their journals because they are both useful and memorable.
- Here are a few examples of student couplets to inspire you to challenge your students to write a few original couplets:

> Spurred by his wife, by the weird sisters fooled,
> Macbeth was cursed throughout the land he ruled.

> Infinitives, participles, and gerunds are schizophrenic:
> Part verb/part noun/part adjective/part adverb. Frantic!

> Thin, colorful and transparent layers
> Crystallizing in monoclinic forms. Mica!

> Give me a K for Kalium;
> That's the symbol for potassium.

- After giving a recent workshop on active learning to teachers, I asked the assembled group to boil down my presentation into a couplet. Here are a couple of results:

> To change the channel, simply turn
> On education: active learn.

> No more marking, hip hip hooray!
> Active learning – the only way!

Mnemonics

- Request students to come up with a mnemonic for the class to help them remember some important fact about the material to be learned. You might give them a few examples to get them thinking "mnemonically" and await their results: Every Good Boy Deserves Fun for the lines of a musical staff (EGBDF); Lop off the E in Develop(e); World Health Organization (WHO); Richard of York Gave Battle In Vain (the colors of the spectrum – red, orange, yellow, green, blue, indigo, violet), and your own favorites.
- Post the results around the room for all students to enjoy. Encourage students to copy useful mnemonics into their journals.

Crossword Puzzles

- Who has not done a crossword puzzle from the daily newspaper? Making up a crossword is much more difficult than doing one, but it results in a good form of synthesis after students complete a body of work. You might ask small groups to make up a crossword together. When students get stuck, and they will, give them a way out. For example, if students have several good words across and down, but in one spot they have ended up with "PLND" going down, they might give the following clue for a story set during World War II: "In 1939 Hitler invaded _ o _ a _ _." This device – although anathema to crossword purists – will prevent students from bogging down.
- Duplicate crossword puzzles. Having students complete crossword puzzles composed by other students provides a useful review of a body of material.

Acrostics

- Building an acrostic, based on the name of a personality from course material, will make a historical figure, scientist, artist, or author memorable. You can ask students to build the acrostic using only adjectives or you might ask them to include a sentence for every letter. Before assigning an Acrostic with course content, you might have students build one using your name, or their own names. For example:

> **J**udgmental
> **O**verly ambitious
> **H**onorable
> **N**it-picky

Visual Products

Teacher Preparation: None required.
Length of Time: Usually assign this project for homework.

- Students feel a great sense of accomplishment when given the opportunity to demonstrate their comprehension of a body of material through a visual product.
- For students who are not visually accomplished, you might assign several choices to accommodate their different talents: written, a combination of written and visual, or visual-only assignments. Some visual assignments that you might consider adapting:
    - assume you are filming a chapter from the book you are studying. Present a storyboard (with dialogue)
    - convert a chapter from the text into a comic strip
    - design a book jacket for a book you are reading (include advertising blurbs, quotations, photos, etc.)
    - draw a map of the main character's journey, indicating clearly where each main event takes place

- Other students enjoy studying visual products. Because they are familiar with the learned material, they can appreciate the content of the visual products and can be very good judges of the value of the assignment.
- Visual products work very well across the grades and curriculum, giving students opportunities to blend their artistic talents and the learned material in assignments requiring cartoons, comic strips, book jackets, storyboards, visual how-to manuals, maps, graphs, even models and three-dimensional products.
- Instead of asking students to write a research essay, you might ask them to make a family shield (See Chapter 14). As an extension of the Shield Project, you might have students select a literary character, historical personality, author, world leader, or another personality relevant to course content and make a family shield for that personality. On completion, students can present their shields with a short explanatory introduction. You can post the shields for all students to study and enjoy.

Plastinary

Teacher Preparation: Have some plasticine available.
Length of Time: 15 minutes.

- Divide the class into groups of six. Divide each group of six in half so that they can compete in Plastinary the same way they would in Pictionary, except they will have to sculpt the answer instead of drawing it.
- Each threesome in each group should make up a few cards that relate to a body of learned material with a different word to test knowledge, comprehension, or analysis. After they have completed ten cards, they should be ready to play Plastinary.
- One person from the opposing side picks one card, reads it, and within one minute sculpts the plasticine into the clue word. The other two try to guess the word within the time limit. Make up the specific rules to fit your needs.

Board Games

Teacher Preparation: Not much required. Just suggest that students might synthesize a particular unit by devising a board game, and watch the results.

Length of Time: Usually the playing of the game will be part of a larger presentation.

- If you insist that students do not stand at the front reading notes to other students when they make a presentation, they will often devise a board game and either play one game to involve all the class or play several games with small groups.
- In a post-viewing film workshop during one of my classes, a group divided the class into two teams and brought out a 4' x 6' board game with a large foam die. They asked questions, the team conferred for 30 seconds, and a spokesperson gave the answer. If the answer was right, the spokesperson rolled the die and moved the marker accordingly. The usual "move ahead three spaces" and "move back 5 spaces" and "roll an extra time" appeared on the board.
- If you give them the chance, your students will devise many extremely useful and enjoyable board games.

Game Shows

Teacher Preparation: Not much required. Just suggest the material below and see what your students come up with.

Length of Time: 30 minutes of class time for preparation, but students will spend out-of-school time to prepare props.

- With the abundance of game shows on TV, students are bound to be familiar with some of them. You might suggest that they blend part of the course content with an existing TV game show, or invent one of their own.
- After allowing students to work a few days independently to come up with an original synthesis, have them meet in groups of four or five. Have each share his/her game show idea with the others in the group. After they have presented ideas, each group should decide to refine, reform, and revise the chosen show to a point that they can introduce it to the rest of the class (who will act as contestants). The members of the group will act as host(s), producer, director, and general gofers to ensure the smooth running of the show. The group may decide to videotape the show for future playback.
- During one of my classes, a group developed "Name That Character." A host and three guests (with brown paper bags over their heads) appeared. Each guest represented a different character from the novel we'd just studied. The studio audience (class) had to figure out the identity of each guest. The host invited studio audience members to ask the guests questions about their personalities (although they were not allowed to ask questions directly related to the plot of the novel). Questions ranged from "Guest No. 2, what would you do if you were to meet...? Guest No. 1, would you do the same thing? Guest No. 3, what do you think of...? If you had your choice, where, other than the setting in this novel, would you like to live? Why?" By the end of the show, all of the studio audience had identified the guests. As the host stood ready to whip the bag off the head of each guest, he invited the audience to, "Name That Character!" and the class dutifully called out "Serena Joy," then, "the Commander," and finally, "Offred" – all from *The Handmaid's Tale*.

• Game Shows don't just introduce a lot of fun into the active-learning classroom; they also allow students rather than teachers to make up questions in order to test the knowledge, understanding, and appreciation of the course content. You can easily introduce game shows into any grade across the curriculum.

Film Synthesis

Teacher Preparation: None necessary.
Length of Time: Done as a homework assignment, but in small groups.

• For many courses, it seems natural to blend printed fiction and nonfiction and film and give assignments such as, "Film one of the poems from the poetry text." "Film this experiment." "Create a TV game show based on the unit we've been studying."
• Although more and more families have their own camcorders, you might invite someone from your school's audio/visual department to demonstrate the use of a camcorder for the whole class to ensure that everyone knows how to use the equipment. (Chapter 12 also contains information about working on video productions.)
• You can apply the details of the following model workshop to any film synthesis project. Duplicate it or amend to fit your needs.

Film a Poem

Form groups of five. Appoint a director who will be responsible to direct the other four in the group in bringing the poem to life on film. Although the groups should have plenty of discussion and rehearsal time, it should be the director's responsibility to give the final product focus and unity.

For the project, I suggest that you present the poem early in the film so that the viewers experience it pleasurably. You can do this by reading the poem to camera (from memory) in a group or solo or take turns from stanza to stanza. You can even use voiceover techniques while the camera films relevant scenes.

Afterwards, you should connect the poem with the different levels of the thinking process: knowledge, comprehension, analysis, application, evaluation, and synthesis.

Total length of the film must be 10 minutes. The director will lose marks if the film is more than 30 seconds under or over 10 minutes.

On a given day, we will view each 10-minute film. You will be asked to discuss, evaluate, and even grade each one.

• From this experience, students will learn a number of valuable personal lessons:
  – the importance of cooperation
  – seeing and hearing themselves on film
  – working to deadlines
  – learning film techniques
• Students will doubtless enjoy the studied material, in a way that you would not be able to present it to them in the classroom. Their films will often shed new light on the material that never would have occurred to you.

• For the last three terms, it has become commonplace for a few students in my literature classes to make career changes and enrol in a film school at the end of term. When an active-learning project helps a student come to such an important decision, it says a great deal for hands-on education.

Note: When I first began the Film Synthesis project, camcorders were not popular; therefore, I did all the filming of the presentations. The directors were in charge of the various shots, and I acted solely as the director's cameraman. All shooting schedules were completed during half an hour of class time. (I could film two 10-minute productions in one class period.) During my most recent term, out of 12 assignments, I filmed none; students either booked the equipment from the audio/visual department or used their own. I gave one class period for filming, but directors' ambitions often exceeded mine and they took their cast and crew to various locations during weekends and evenings.

YOUR IDEAS FOR SYNTHESIS WORKSHOPS

LAST WORDS

When I graduated from grade twelve, I thought I was pretty clever; when I received my BA, I felt quite nervous about my lack of knowledge; and when I received my MA, I knew how limited my knowledge really was. During most of my teaching career, I presented myself as the authority figure in the classroom, and I was always afraid that my ignorance would be exposed. I didn't like to admit that some of my students were more intelligent than I – not as experienced, but certainly more intelligent. Many times these students challenged me, but luckily I managed to escape with only a few minor bruises to my ego. I worked harder to master the course content so that only I knew the mysteries of all the literature on my reading lists.

Not until I changed my teaching approach from a presentational to an environmental one did I feel truly comfortable in my chosen profession. It now matters little to me that some students are more intelligent than I, for I have established a classroom learning community that allows each student to learn, meet challenges, solve problems, and develop their higher-level cognitive thinking skills.

It's now very difficult for me to paint a negative picture of active learning. After all, I'm convinced that it works better than the traditional lecture method where students sit passively and learn little. I feel I am qualified to pass judgment on both methods because I spent so much of my career being the dominant authority in the room, rightly or wrongly making my students dependent on me and *my* thinking processes. Teaching year after year was just like putting the same old record on to PLAY. Classes never varied much. Discussions arose, but I managed to ensure that all my students learned how to think according to the "collective knowledge of the scholars." Now, classes are filled with variety. Each section of the same course produces a unique learning experience. What works in one classroom will not necessarily work in another, and by being flexible, I am able to identify and refine students' strengths in all classes. By releasing students from the confines of traditional education practices, I have been surprised beyond my expectations.

The high point for me and one of my literature classes during a recent term was a Film Synthesis presentation. The text we used for the course, *Understanding Movies* by Louis Giannetti, suggests that students analyze a short scene from a movie of their choice according to a list of characteristics. Seven fellows, who at the beginning of the term were definitely low achievers, chose to do the "Grease Lightning" scene from the movie *Grease*. They showed the scene from the movie to the class and then, roleplaying as characters from a tough gang, analyzed it in great detail. The textbook suggested that the group rerun the scene to the class so that they would appreciate it on second viewing. Instead, these seven flipped on the buttons of a sound system they had set up before the class began, played the recording of "Grease Lightning," lip-synched the words, and offered a well-staged, choreographed presentation. The class gave them a standing ovation.

Low achievers, paradoxically, respond better to active learning, at least at the beginning of the term, than high achievers. High achievers have learned how to play the game of education. They quickly zero in on the instructor's methods, respond to discussion questions, ask leading questions, offer a few insights, know how to conduct office visitations, and have no difficulty acing the course. At first, high achievers flounder in active-learning workshops; they want to escape rather than sharing what they know about the subject with lesser mortals. Once they begin to work in groups with other high achievers, however, they learn (with little guidance from the teacher) to challenge each other and dig into the course content in a much deeper, richer way than they thought possible. They quickly learn that they will get more out of the course if they put more into it. And, as a result, they spend far more time working on their studies than trying to outwit their teachers.

Of the hundreds of student testimonials I have received, the following two will give you an idea about the pros and cons of active learning:

Ross entered the class as a low achiever.

I have a low self-esteem and usually do not like to associate with people. If I am ever standing up in front of people and talking, I am usually a nervous wreck; however, during the 1987 fall semester at Langara College, one course, English 230, changed my life considerably.

When I first walked into my English 230 class early one morning in September, I almost died. The entire class was sitting in a circle calling out each other's names. I forced myself to join the group knowing that I would soon transfer out of the class. As time went on, our class frequently broke up into several groups and I started to meet more and more people. After a while, I really enjoyed being a part of a new group and meeting new people. Now I was a little more at ease when it came to meeting new people. Often, we would have to get up and express ourselves whether it be in some kind of role playing or simply reciting something. The more and more I got up in front of everyone the easier and more relaxed I became. At first, I was very nervous and shy; I would often break out in a total sweat. My last incident where I had to express myself was when our group presented a film synthesis. Even though everyone will surely say I looked nervous, I was not. For the first part, yes, but the last part, no way. Being more confident and relaxed in front of people is one way I have changed in English 230...

Rachel entered class as a precocious high achiever.

Embarking on English 230 at the beginning of this term, I had envisioned a highly personal sorting-through of all the works to be assigned, and looked forward to cloistering myself away in order to arrive at unsullied kernels of truth regarding those assigned works. I have emerged from the course with a new respect and admiration for my fellows and a decreased feeling of alienation from and for them, surprisingly due to the form of group learning and sharing of ideas that was promoted in the course.

At the beginning of the term I felt very protective of my precious ideas and was reluctant in sharing them with members of the class. I felt very threatened by the format of the lessons, which required much public display of things I held to be very personal and feared a sort of watering-down of my own strengths would take place. To combat this, I strongly asserted my ideas in any group situation that was required and did enough work to warrant the predominance of my ideas in any project I was part of. Later in the term, I found that the groups I was in still accomplished and carried out projects to a standard I was pleased with. This made me see the error of my ways: my rigidity and perfectionism were not born of a desire to get the group the highest possible mark, but out of a lack of faith in my peers which I now see is part of much that I do not like about myself. In the final group projects in which I took part there was much vigorous discussion and I learned more than in previous projects. I learned to put faith in other people and be secure in the knowledge that we are all just folk!

I would like to thank the professor who abided my attitude problem for many months. Thank you.

In conclusion, you will discover that in an active-learning classroom "the teacher does not teach, but simply provides an opportunity for students to learn" (Albert Einstein).

ALPHABETICAL LIST OF WORKSHOPS

Dear Reader:

If you are finding *Workshops for Active Learning* useful, tell some of your colleagues and friends about it. Or let us have their names and addresses and we will send them information. The text should be useful for anyone who would like to give up lecturing to a group of passive listeners and, instead, involve them actively:

* elementary, junior and high-school teachers
* college and university professors
* conference and keynote speakers
* ministers and Sunday-school teachers
* all kinds of job trainers for small and large corporations
* teachers and counsellors in recreational centers, hospitals, playschools, etc.

For your convenience, use the order form below. Thank you.

✂ --

JFP Productions presents

Workshops for Active Learning by John F. Parker

(a handbook with over 200 practical workshops for teachers)

Are you looking for an alternative to lecturing? IF SO, complete and send this order form to JFP Productions, PO Box 1953, Pt. Roberts, WA 98281-1953 or
JFP Productions, #1203 - 1111 Haro St., Vancouver, BC V6E 1E3
or FAX Purchase Order to (604) 689-1279 or E-mail to John_Parker@mindlink.bc.ca

Amount

☐ *Workshops for Active Learning* **$19.95**   _____

☐ **Computer Disk containing 75 student handouts to use with the text**
    ☐ *for PC* ☐ *for MAC*   **$10.50**   _____

☐ **Postage and Handling ($4.00)**   _____

                                    Subtotal   _____
                          7% GST *(Canadian orders)* _____

TOTAL *(Enclose cheque or money order or purchase order number.)*   _____

Please: Make cheque or money order out to John F. Parker

☐ *Send me information about one- or two-day workshops conducted by the author.*

Name (please print) _____
Address _____
City _____ *Prov. or State* _____ *Zip* _____
Subject or Grade that you teach _____

PRODUCTIONS

11149 Prospect Drive
Delta, BC, Canada
V4E 2R4   (604) 594-1832

P.O. Box 1953
't. Roberts, WA
98281-1953

Dear Reader:

If you are finding *Workshops for Active Learning* useful, tell some of your colleagues and friends about it. Or let us have their names and addresses and we will send them information. The text should be useful for anyone who would like to give up lecturing to a group of passive listeners and, instead, involve them actively:

- elementary, junior and high school teachers
- college and university professors
- conference and keynote speakers
- ministers and Sunday-school teachers
- all kinds of job trainers for small and large corporations
- teachers and counsellors in recreational centers, hospitals, playschools,etc.

For your convenience, use the order form below.

Thank you.

✂ ---

JFP Productions presents
Workshops for Active Learning
(a text with over 200 practical workshops for teachers)

Are you looking for an alternative to lecturing? IF SO, complete and send this order form to JFP Productions, PO Box 1953, Pt. Roberts, WA 98281-1953
                    or   11149 Prospect Drive, Delta, BC V4E 2R4.

                                                                      Amount

❏ *Workshops for Active Learning* ($19.95)   _____
❏ Loose, unbound, 3-holed version ($19.95)   _____
❏ Postage and handling ($2.00 in US; $3.00 in Canada)   _____
❏ Computer disk containing 75 of the student workshops
        to use with the text. ($5.50)   _____
    ❏ for WordPerfect (MS-DOS)
    ❏ for Microsoft Word 4 (Mac osh)
                            Send eck or money order for   _____

Send me information about
❏ quantity discounts   ❏ one- or two-day workshops,
                                     conducted by the author.

Name (please print) _____

Address _____

City _____   Prov. or State_____ Zip _____